Giorgio de Chirico

Giorgio de Chirico, Rome, October 1949. *Herbert List photograph*

Giorgio de Chirico

BY JAMES THRALL SOBY

THE MUSEUM OF MODERN ART   NEW YORK

REPRINT EDITION, 1966   PUBLISHED FOR
THE MUSEUM OF MODERN ART BY ARNO PRESS

Published by the Museum of Modern Art, New York
All rights reserved
Library of Congress Catalog Card Number 55—5422
Designed by Edward L. Mills
Second Reprint 1968—Arno Press, Inc., New York
Manufactured in the United States of America

Contents

Acknowledgments

The revision of the first version of this book, published in 1941 as *The Early Chirico*, has occupied the writer at intervals since 1945. At the conclusion of the recent war the most urgent task in research was to try to assemble theretofore unavailable material on de Chirico's art and career in Italy, his fatherland and central inspiration. In that country I met with generous cooperation and lively interest in the subject of this book. At Milan Virginio Ghiringelli, Lamberto Vitali and Raffaele Carrieri supplied valuable information about the artist, as did the late Alberto Savinio, de Chirico's younger brother. In the same city Giovanni Scheiwiller has been of immense help, giving me otherwise unobtainable books and articles from his personal library and also the unique series of photographs, here published on pages 19 to 21, of paintings executed by de Chirico in 1909 and long since repainted or lost. The Milanese collector, R. Toninelli, has been of great assistance on many occasions, acting as gracious host, arranging interviews with critics and fellow-collectors and accompanying the writer on long excursions in search of existing prototypes for elements appearing in de Chirico's early iconography—notably the piazzas and Victorian statuary of Turin. Signor Toninelli has been an indispensable ally in the long preparation of this book.

At Venice Rodolfo Pallucchini, Secretary General of the Biennale di Venezia, and Umbro Apollonio, Curator of the Biennale's Archives on the History of Contemporary Art, have put their documentary resources at my disposal and otherwise been extremely helpful. In Florence Carlo L. Ragghianti supplied out-of-print copies of the magazine, *Critica d'Arte*, of which he is the distinguished editor, and spared time for informative conversations about de Chirico's art.

At Rome Giorgio Castelfranco, one of de Chirico's earliest patrons and champions in Italy, supplied firsthand recollections of the painter, dating back to the years immediately following the First World War. Similarly the noted poet, Giuseppe Ungaretti, received the writer warmly and in a subsequent correspondence has clarified many points about de Chirico's early career; it was he who took charge of the paintings the artist left in his Paris studio on his departure for Italy in 1915 and who helped interest his French friends and colleagues, André Breton and Paul Eluard, in these paintings.

De Chirico's first one-man exhibition in Italy was held at the gallery of Anton Giulio Bragaglia very early in 1919. In conversations and letters Signor Bragaglia has recalled important facts relating to the exhibition and has given the writer a transcript of a rare article by de Chirico, *Noi Metafisici*, published on February 15, 1919, in *Cronache d'Attualità*, the organ of Bragaglia's gallery, known as *L'Epoca*. Italo Faldi, whose book, *Il Primo de Chirico* (1949), was the first monograph in Italian to deal with the artist's paintings of 1910—18 as a separate entity within the latter's career, offered helpful advice, as did Lionello Venturi. And the widow of the late Mario Broglio, once of Rome and the publisher there of many of de Chirico's most important articles and works of art in *Valori Plastici*, has answered promptly inquiries first addressed to her husband.

From 1911 to 1915 de Chirico worked in Paris and produced some of the finest pictures of his early career. It therefore seemed important to accumulate as much information as possible about these first years of his maturity as an artist. Mlle Mauricette Fallek acted as an extremely efficient research assistant in the French capital and traced many vital documents relating to the painter's relationship with the great poet and critic, Guillaume Apollinaire, who more than anyone may be said to have "discovered" de Chirico. Marcel Adéma, the leading authority on Apollinaire's life and work, was unfailingly helpful, and the poet's widow has kindly answered by letter innumerable questions about the apartment on the Boulevard St. Germain where she and Apollinaire lived and which she has preserved devotedly all these years since his tragic death in 1918.

The writer is also indebted to Marc Vaux, who photographed many of the de Chirico paintings and drawings remaining in Parisian collections, usually in their owners' apartments under difficult lighting conditions. I am particularly grateful to the late Paul Eluard, who just before his recent death persuaded his friend, Pablo Picasso, to relinquish the transcript of an early de Chirico manuscript, here published in English (except for the short poems by the artist which are virtually impossible to translate) as Appendix A. A fervent admirer of de Chirico's early work, Paul Eluard was consistently helpful in other ways and always showed a warm interest in the preparation of this book. A second de Chirico manuscript of c.1913 was made available by Jean Paulhan of the NRF, surrealism's chief publisher, and the owner of several major works of the artist's first Paris years; the manuscript is printed here as Appendix B. The writer's admiration for de Chirico's paintings and drawings of 1910—18 was first aroused by André Breton's book, *Le surréalisme et la peinture*, published in 1928 and still a central source of reference. M. Breton encouraged the preparation of *The Early Chirico* and also the present, completely revised monograph on the Italian painter. Thanks also are due to Bernard Poissonnier, who allowed me to have made in Switzerland new negatives of his many de Chiricos; to Marcel Raval; M. le Vicomte de Noailles; the eminent critic, G. di San Lazzaro; Daniel-Henry Kahnweiler; and Mme S. Gille-Delafon, Secretary of the International Association of Art Critics in Paris. The writer has enjoyed and profited immensely from a long correspondence about de Chirico with René Gaffé of Brussels, one of the most courageous and perceptive collectors and critics of modern art in all Europe.

Among English enthusiasts for de Chirico's early art, Roland Penrose has repeatedly furnished useful information; his personal collection of this art was for years the most extensive in Europe. Thanks must be expressed, too, to Geoffrey Grigson, Arthur Jeffress, Peter Watson, Edward James, Douglas Cooper and especially E. L. T. Mesens, whose exhibitions of de Chirico's paintings and drawings of 1910—18 have done much to establish the latter's fame in London and who has consistently championed the early works of the Italian artist, not only in England but in his (Mesens') native Belgium.

Fridtzof Zschokke, Assistant Director of the Kunstmuseum at Basel, kindly arranged to have the de Chirico's in Bernard Poissonnier's collection photographed when they were on loan to the Kunstmuseum in 1949, and also furnished excellent photographs of paintings by Arnold Böcklin which exerted a profound influence on de Chirico in youth. Eberhard Hanfstaengl, Director of the Bavarian Art Museums in Munich, forwarded the sad information that all records of the Munich Academy, where de Chirico was trained as an artist, were destroyed by fire during the recent war. In 1950 Fabian Linden, then a member of the ECA Mission to Austria, helped diligently in the futile search for de Chirico pictures of the early period which have disappeared in Central Europe. And in October of the same year Alfred Kubin wrote from Wernstein in Austria, where he has lived and worked since 1906, the reply to my inquiry regarding his Chiricoesque drawing, *Vision of Italy* (1904—05); part of his reply is here reprinted as a footnote to page 30.

In America my greatest debt is to Alfred H. Barr, Jr., who has made innumerable suggestions as to the contents of the text and encouraged its publication with steadfast interest. The translations of Italian quotations are the skilled work of Edith M. Weinberger and Margaret Scolari; the early manuscripts in French by de Chirico (Appendices A and B) were admirably translated by Louise Bourgeois and Robert Goldwater. Sheldon and Caroline Keck, restorers of paintings for the Brooklyn Museum and the Museum of Modern Art, have provided invaluable technical analyses of de Chirico paintings of various dates. Their photographer, Charles Uht, made an extensive series of photographs for the writer, using such techniques as X-ray, infra-red and macrophotography, and revealing important evidence on questions of dating and change in de Chirico's art. Some of this documentary evidence is here published on pages 126—128; the rest is available in the library of the Museum of Modern Art. Bernard Karpel, Librarian of the Museum and author of this book's bibliography, has been of tireless help in uncovering scarce material. The author is indebted to Helen M. Franc for her painstaking and devoted work in preparing the index. Pierre Matisse, through whose hands most of the many early de Chirico paintings in this country have passed, has made available his detailed knowledge of these paintings, as he did when *The Early Chirico* was in preparation.

I am much indebted, too, to Roger Shattuck, a leading American authority on Guillaume Apollinaire and translator of some of the latter's finest poems; to Agnes Mongan for information about de Chirico's picture-restorer friend, Nicola Lochoff, who around 1920 temporarily converted the artist to the tempera medium; to Georgette Passedoit; Peggy Guggenheim; Gisela M. A. Richter, for material regarding the Roman copy of the lost Hellenistic statue of Adriadne which affected de Chirico so deeply in 1913; to Marianne Winter Martin of the Philadelphia Museum; and to Agnes Rindge Claflin, Chairman of the Art Department at Vassar College. Giovanni Girardon, brother of the late Mario Girardon, a partner of Mario Broglio in the firm of *Valori Plastici*, which published and exhibited de Chirico's paintings for a period of years beginning in 1918, has elucidated several details of the loss by fire of *Hermetic Melancholy* (page 240) and possibly other works brought to this country by his brother. Monroe Wheeler, Director of Publications for the Museum of Modern Art, has encouraged the writer throughout the book's preparation; his assistant, Miss Frances Pernas, has shown her customary patience and skill in getting the book to press.

J. T. S.

When most I wink, then do mine eyes best see,
For all the day they view things unsuspected.

SHAKESPEARE

Ce que j'écoute ne vaut rien; il n'y a que ce que
mes yeux voient ouverts et plus encore fermés.

DE CHIRICO, C. 1913

Foreword

In 1941 the first version of this book was published as *The Early Chirico*. It was concerned with de Chirico's career from 1910 through 1917 and reproduced seventy of his paintings from that period.

The present version of the book has been entirely rewritten and differs from the other in many respects. The painter with whose work it deals is referred to throughout as "de Chirico" rather than as "Chirico," the name by which he was internationally known, with his own assent, for almost thirty years. More recently, however, de Chirico has returned to his native Italy and there is widely known by his full name, most particularly as the founder of the *scuola metafisica*, one of the two most influential movements in twentieth-century Italian art, the other being Futurism. Now that de Chirico again paints in Italy rather than in Paris, it seems appropriate to use the name by which his countrymen refer to him. I have a more personal reason for doing so. Reviewing *The Early Chirico* in *Fiera Letteraria* for January 30, 1947, the artist wrote: "Let Signor Soby understand that my name is Giorgio de Chirico and not Chirico." Any man if he prefers is entitled to the name with which he was christened, even though to the world he is better known by another.

The review of *The Early Chirico* I have just mentioned was scathing in its denunciation. But it seems significant that at no point in the review did the painter question the authenticity of any of the seventy pictures reproduced, though this would have been the most damaging charge he could have made. I should add that since the recent war de Chirico in conversations with reporters and friends is said to have disclaimed two or sometimes three of the seventy early paintings.* But one of these he has since authenticated in writing and his opinion of the others has varied according to his mood and

* In December, 1954, while the present volume was at the printer's, de Chirico visited the Italian critic, Raffaele Carrieri, in Milan. The latter showed the artist a copy of *The Early Chirico*. On three of the book's plates de Chirico wrote "this picture is false"; a fourth he marked with a question mark. The three paintings thus disclaimed by the artist are: *The Joy of Return* (page 214 in the present volume); *The War* (page 217); and *The Language of a Child* (page 218). The picture inscribed with a question mark by de Chirico is *Politics* (page 220).

I see no valid stylistic, technical or iconographical reason to change my opinion that all four paintings are authentic works of de Chirico's early period, either forgotten by the artist or refuted by him in one of his many moments of irresponsible pique against his own brilliant youth.

audience. I have therefore again reproduced all seventy pictures, while assigning different, and I trust more accurate, dates to some of them.

I have also included early paintings which I had not seen or which were not available for reproduction during the recent war, when the first version of this book was published. The present volume does not pretend to be a *catalogue raisonné* of the pictures de Chirico completed between 1910 and the end of 1917, but it is my firm conviction that extremely few works from these years remain to be found. The book also reproduces and discusses a number of paintings executed after the close of the First World War. Some of these are of decided interest and one of them—*The Sacred Fish* of 1919—is a masterwork in terms both of intrinsic quality and of its influence on other painters, chiefly of surrealist persuasion.

This influence is apparent in the pictures by Ernst, Magritte, Tanguy, Dali and Delvaux, reproduced on pages 149–152. But I have not attempted to trace the influence in a separate section of the text, as I did in *The Early Chirico*. The subject is complicated and would require a fuller treatment than space allows. For the same reason only a limited number of de Chirico's early drawings have been reproduced, and then primarily because they clarify shifts in his vision, purpose and style as a painter.

J. T. S.

Giorgio de Chirico

PARENTS AND CHILDHOOD: EARLY TRAINING IN ART

Giorgio de Chirico was born on July 10, 1888, "during a torrid day,"[1] at Volo, capital of the coastal province of Thessaly in Greece. From this seaport, according to legend, the Argonauts had sailed in quest of the Golden Fleece. De Chirico's childhood was partly spent there, partly in Athens. He was the second of three children. His sister died as a very young girl; his brother Andrea, known professionally until his recent death as Alberto Savinio, was three years his junior. His parents were Italian, his father having come from Palermo, his mother from Genoa.

The de Chirico family had settled in Greece because the father, Evariste, was an engineer for the Thessalian railroad lines, then under construction. With that aristocratic pride which has been so important a factor in his maturity, de Chirico tells us that his father "of his entire family of gentlemen was the only one who had wished to work."[2]

Evariste de Chirico's profession was of exceptional relevance to the art his son was to create between the years 1910 and 1918. Indeed it would be difficult to think of another artist, old or modern, in whose work childhood memories of a parent's occupation play so central a part. Trains are a recurrent iconographical element in the de Chirico paintings known collectively as "the Italian squares" or the "memories of Italy." They disturb the ancient silences as real trains must have done in fact when winding through the Thessalian hills, following Evariste de Chirico's plans. If it was the father's function to penetrate deep space in a practical sense, it was one of the son's most remarkable achievements as an artist that he revived far perspective and made of it an evocative poetic instrument. The word "engineer" occurs frequently in the titles of de Chirico's early pictures; one of the most eloquent of his short prose pieces is called "The Son of the Engineer."[3] Moreover, draftsmen's tools are to be found time and again in his paintings of 1913–17, while in many cases the geometric disposition of forms seems related, however obliquely, to the sketches and mechanical drawing instruments which must have littered the elder de Chirico's desk.

But what was the emotional relationship between father and son? We know only that it must have been unusually intense. It could not otherwise have resulted in what is surely one of the most powerful and obsessive of de Chirico's images—*The Child's Brain* (page 193), in which the father's mustachioed authority over the family is suggested with extraordinary force. Throughout his earlier career the painter seems to have been profoundly moved by the memory of his father. When, for example, de Chirico was asked by the surrealists in 1924 to describe the dream that had impressed him most, he wrote:

> I struggle in vain with the man whose eyes are suspicious and very gentle. Each time I grasp him, he frees himself by quietly spreading his arms, which have an unbelievable strength, an incalculable power. They are like irresistible levers, like all-powerful machines, like those gigantic cranes which raise from the swarming shipyards whole quarters of floating fortresses, with turrets as heavy as antediluvian mammals. I struggle in vain with the man of suspicious and very gentle glance. From each grasp, however frenzied it be, he frees himself easily, laughing and barely raising his arms... It is my father who thus appears to me in my dreams, and yet when I look at him he is not at all as he was when I saw him alive in the time of my childhood. Nevertheless, it is he. There is something *far off* in the whole expression of his face, something which perhaps existed when I saw him alive and which now, after more than twenty years, strikes me with full force when I see him again in a dream.[4]

This description was written at a time when de Chirico was strongly, if briefly, attracted to the surrealists' Freudian premise. More recently, in his autobiography, the artist has given us a more direct account of his father:

> My father was a man of the nineteenth century; he was an architectural engineer and he was also an old-fashioned gentleman; brave, loyal, intelligent, hard-working and good... Like many of his contemporaries he had many skills; he was a first-class engineer, his handwriting was beautiful, he drew well, he had a fine ear for music, he was an acute and ironic observer, he hated injustice, loved animals, he treated the wealthy and powerful haughtily but always came to the defense of the weak and the poor. He was a good horseman, he had engaged in several pistol duels...[5]

De Chirico's autobiography includes numerous other warm and proud references to his father. At one point, however, the painter remarks: "Despite a deep mutual affection, the relationship between my father and myself was somewhat distant and cold. A certain reticence prevented us from indulging in the demonstrative behavior of the middle classes."[6]

The artist's autobiographical references to his mother are less frequent, and it seems probable that when the children were young she was closer to the younger son, Andrea—"My brother was 'the handsome one' of the family and our mother was very proud of him."[7] Perhaps not until the death of the father in 1905, when de Chirico was seventeen, did the mother's influence over her older son become the strong force which is vividly commemorated in the 1919 *Portrait of the Artist with His Mother* (page 137).

The two parents appear to have been equally interested in encouraging both boys' talents. The father gave de Chirico his first instruction in drawing, showing him how

14

to copy a portrait with the aid of ruled crosses; the mother admired her older son's sketches and bought him books on draftsmanship. Around 1897, after several years in Athens, the de Chirico family moved back to Volo. There Giorgio was provided with an art teacher. His name was Mavrudis. He was a Greek from Trieste and de Chirico described him in his autobiography as immensely gifted and in matters of theoretic discussion comparable to Ruskin. Mavrudis gave de Chirico drawing lessons three times a week until in 1899 the family again moved to Athens. In that city Mavrudis was replaced as instructor by an Italian artist, Carlo Barbieri, whom de Chirico mentions as being far less talented than his predecessor and further accuses of having had extreme halitosis.

In Athens de Chirico was tutored in languages, took lessons on the 'cello, saw his first exhibition of paintings in which he especially admired some scenes of the recently concluded Greek-Turkish war by one Roilós. (To this day de Chirico considers Roilós to have been a better painter than Giovanni Fattori, whom most of his countrymen regard as one of the best late nineteenth-century Italian artists.) He also took additional lessons in drawing from a Swiss named Gilleron and studied other subjects at the *Liceo Leonino*, a Catholic seminary. In brief his education was thorough and strict, a fact which in his older age he approves to such a degree that, with characteristic violence, he dismisses more progressive educational methods as "related to a certain mentality common to nudists and vegetarians."[8]

Around 1900 de Chirico was enrolled by his parents in the drawing classes at the Polytechnic Institute in Athens. The instruction given him there was traditional, arduous—and slow. Four years of copying prints, drawings and finally casts of sculpture were required before the student progressed to the living model and, at last, to the use of color. But de Chirico had apparently already begun to experiment with oil painting at home. He was then twelve years old. His first painting was a still life of lemons and he was advised in technique by Bolonakis, a member of the Polytechnic staff. He eventually entered the painting classes at the Polytechnic, where his instructor was a man named Jacobidis, of whom he still speaks respectfully. Late in 1905 or early in 1906 de Chirico graduated from the Polytechnic's art school, extensively trained in technical procedures.

MUNICH

In 1905 Evariste de Chirico died after a long illness. His widow presently decided to move with the boys to Munich. Her choice of the Bavarian city was perhaps dictated by Andrea's musical talents, for the younger son had shown decided ability while studying at the Athens Conservatory. We should remember, however, that Munich at the turn of the century was considered a rival to Paris in the plastic arts, at least in provincial circles. Gemma de Chirico probably favored Munich as being both more accessible than Paris and as the one city in Europe where she felt both sons could be trained adequately, Andrea in music, Giorgio in painting. At any rate the family set off for Germany in 1906, stopping on the way at Venice, where de Chirico was not deeply impressed by the art of Titian, Tintoretto or Veronese. The family also stopped briefly at Milan, where Giorgio was stirred by the pictures of Segantini and Previati—almost certainly the most advanced works he had seen up to that date.

At Munich de Chirico enrolled in the Academy of Fine Arts and studied there throughout his two-year stay in the German city. Writing his autobiography in long retrospect, he claims to have disliked the Bavarians and to have made only two German friends, both Prussian. As to his opinion of the Academy, it has been typically inconsistent. At times, especially when inveighing against the School of Paris, he has defended it proudly. Then again he has compared it unfavorably to the Polytechnic at Athens—"Not a soul at the Academy could handle charcoal or brush."[9] At the time, he adds, the Academy was dominated by the Secession, whose style he holds responsible for what he considers to have been one of the two most disastrous aspects of contemporary civilization: "Modern Painting and Nazism."[10] We shall come later to a discussion of de Chirico's fanatical hatred of modern art, of which he was once one of the most influential progenitors, but it may be noted in passing that none of his diatribes is more absurd than this.

ARNOLD BÖCKLIN

Unfortunately it is impossible to give details of de Chirico's studies at the Munich Academy, since its files were entirely destroyed by fire during the recent war, according to a letter received from Dr. Eberhard Hanfstaengl.* In any case, it was outside the Academy's classrooms that de Chirico found the greatest single source of inspiration for his own early career—the painting of the Swiss-German, Arnold Böcklin. More adept at languages than his brother, de Chirico used to accompany Andrea to the latter's music lessons at the house of the composer and organist, Max Reger. He declares: "When I did not have to translate into Italian the professor's remarks, I would leaf through a large album of magnificent prints of Böcklin's paintings."[11] These paintings paved the way for one of those curious reversals of direction which are not uncommon in the history of art. Whereas Böcklin had evolved an essentially Germanic kind of painting from an Italianate vision, de Chirico was presently to create a thoroughly Italian art from a German metaphysical premise.

* On Feb. 15, 1950, Dr. Eberhard Hanfstaengl wrote to Curt Valentin as follows: "Unfortunately all the files of the Academy of Arts have been entirely destroyed by fire; therefore it is impossible to do any research about de Chirico in regard to when he studied in Munich."

16

Signora de Chirico, with Giorgio and Andrea,
Greece, c. 1897 (from *Aria d'Italia*, no. 2,
May, 1940, Milan, Edizioni Daria Guarnati)

Evariste and Gemma de Chirico, with their two sons,
Giorgio and Andrea, Greece, c. 1897 (from *Aria d'Italia*,
no. 2, May, 1940. Milan, Edizioni Daria Guarnati)

17

Böcklin: *Battle of the Centaurs*, 1873. Kunstmuseum, Basel

Böcklin: *Odysseus and Calypso*, 1881–83. Kunstmuseum, Basel

De Chirico: *The Battle Between the Hoplites and the Centaurs*, 1909

De Chirico: *Seascape*, 1909

De Chirico: *Seascape with Mermaid*, 1909

De Chirico: *Landscape*, 1909

20

De Chirico: *The Dying Centaur*, 1909

De Chirico: *Landscape*, 1909

Klinger: Plate II from *Paraphrase on the Finding of a Glove*, Berlin, 1881. Etching, $11^3/_4$ x $8^1/_4$"

Klinger: Plate VII from *Paraphrase on the Finding of a Glove*, Berlin, 1881. Etching, $5^5/_8$ x $10^9/_{16}$"

22

Klinger: Plate VIII from *Paraphrase on the Finding of a Glove*, Berlin, 1881. Etching, $5^5/_8 \times 10^1/_2''$

Kubin: *Vision of Italy*, c. 1904–05. Colored drawing

23

The Church of Santa Croce, Florence. Alinari photograph

De Chirico: *Portrait of Andrea de Chirico* (Alberto Savinio), 1910

Just a few years before de Chirico's arrival in Munich, the aged Böcklin had died at his villa near Florence. To the Tuscan peasants his massive frame and bulbous face had suggested the nickname, "Bismarck." But they had apparently never used the nickname comfortably even among themselves. The artist's behavior had suggested peculiarities of character that belied so facile a description. Toward the end of his life, for example, Böcklin had sat for hours in his garden, paralyzed and near death, but holding to his ears great sea shells so as to hear the roar of an ocean he could no longer visit. He had talked incessantly of a flying machine and littered his house with plans for its construction. He was a painter, but he had walked unseeing through a countryside which most visiting artists thought God-sent for art's purpose. A few natives had seen him work. They reported that sometimes he painted in a frenzy, swift and intent, but that often he sat before a canvas for days on end, swaying in his chair, his eyes closed. To the Tuscans, used to ordinary landscapists from the North, this had been a curious way for an artist to behave. They must have wondered what manner of painter Böcklin was.

The young Giorgio de Chirico could have given them a more perceptive answer than his instructors at the Munich Academy (though not necessarily a more enthusiastic one, since the *avant-garde* reaction against Böcklin's art, typified by Meier-Graefe's virulent attack, had just begun). For de Chirico, Böcklin had been a painter whose technique was so exceptional that it made the real appear unreal, the unreal real. He had been, that is to say, the kind of artist whom the German critic, Franz Roh, described in the mid-1920s as a "magic realist"—a painter for whom precision of execution was an instrument of fantastic suggestion. Certainly one of Böcklin's main accomplishments was to give fantasy the quick believability of everyday occurrence. This aspect of his art attracted de Chirico most, as is altogether clear in the latter's article on Böcklin published in *Il Convegno* in 1920.

The impact of surprise [de Chirico wrote] is especially strong in Böcklin's painting, *The Centaur at the Blacksmith's*. The vision must have hit him suddenly. The classic solemnity of the composition enhances the strangeness of the subject. Peasants have come with their children to look at the centaur, and their figures have the ghostlike appearance of certain apparitions in Giotto and Uccello. The body of the centaur is astonishingly realistic. As you look at that perfect creature, who with his hoof on the block shows the blacksmith the work to be done, you do not think at all of the word "monster"; he is a likable person; he is nice...[12]

By the time this article was written, in 1920, de Chirico had been exposed to Guillaume Apollinaire's theory that authentic modern art was distinguishable by the element of "surprise." Yet there can be no doubt that as a youth in Munich he responded directly to the apparitional aspects of Böcklin's art. To make the unlikely seem instantly credible was to become a main preoccupation of de Chirico's entire early career and his *Convegno* article, though published several years after this career had changed its course, typifies his lifelong attitude toward the Swiss-German artist.

25

Böcklin's art had been one of philosophic as opposed to voluptuous sensation, as de Chirico's was to be throughout his youthful years. And some comparison of technical methods may be relevant. In physical terms Böcklin's paintings had been achieved at first through elaborate applications of tempera and varnish, later through an alchemy borrowed in part from the Renaissance masters, partly the result of the artist's own eager research. Yet a paradox of Böcklin's technique was that it tended to hide itself behind metaphysical content; we need only compare him with Manet or the impressionists to see how dominant was his concern with messages of the spirit. De Chirico, too, particularly in his "Italian Squares" of 1912—15, used thin, bland surfaces, without impasto, with no sign whatever of sensual relish in medium.

But what paintings by Böcklin did the young de Chirico admire most? From the evidence of his own paintings and the *Convegno* article, it seems obvious that he preferred those belonging to the middle period, dating from roughly 1864 to 1887. To this period belong such works as *A Villa by the Sea* (1864); *A Rocky Chasm* (1870); the first version of *The Isle of the Dead* (1880), now in the Metropolitan Museum at New York; *The Sacred Grove* (1882); *Prometheus* (1882); *The Silence of the Forest* (1885); *Naiads at Play* (1886) and *An Idyll of the Sea* (1887). It is the period, too, of *In the Trough of the Waves*, which de Chirico calls Böcklin's "greatest canvas,"[13] and of *Odysseus and Calypso* (1881—83) (page 18), whose shrouded figure is so literally quoted in de Chirico's *The Enigma of the Oracle* (page 165) and other early works.

The above-named Böcklin paintings are those in which the artist's full romantic force may be felt; they seem far superior to the pastoral scenes for which he had a weakness during his declining years. Yet even in the best of them there is a marked discrepancy between technical ability and plastic conception, though de Chirico has persistently denied the fact. Böcklin was a gifted painter who seldom transcended the limitations of a literary predilection, long since outworn. He was in fact a belated victim of the close interrelationship among the arts of music, literature and art on which the Romantic movement had insisted. In the hands of lesser figures like Böcklin, this interrelationship ended in a confusion of the boundaries which must always separate the various arts; it arrived at a redundancy and over-statement against which our own century's artists have reacted violently. Böcklin, for example, was a painter whose vision was both excessively dramatic and basically weak, with a resultant leaning toward the operatic or the coy. (His spirit seems Wagnerian, and it is surprising to learn that he disapproved of Wagner's music and refused to design a stage production of it.) Böcklin might have been Holbein's heir. Instead he was the descendant, however talented, of the early nineteenth-century "Nazarenes" and other revivalist groups which tried to disguise Germanic solemnity by a borrowed Italian grace.

Whatever may be the shortcomings of Böcklin's art, it made an overwhelming impression on the young de Chirico, as may be seen in the latter's first serious pictures (pages 19–21). Indeed de Chirico took Böcklin's art as a point of departure from which he moved fairly steadily away during his years at Paris (1911–15) and at Ferrara (1915–18), only to return to the same source in the series of mythological landscapes, also partly inspired by Dosso Dossi, which reached a climax in *The Departure of the Knight Errant* of 1923 (page 141). And finally, a passage in de Chirico's *Convegno* article on Böcklin makes abundantly plain the relationship between the latter's pictures and certain of his own:

> Böcklin's metaphysical power always springs from the precision and definition of a decided apparition. He never painted a fog; he never traced an imprecise contour; in this his classicism and greatness consist... Each of his works evokes that same disconcerting shock of surprise we all feel when we meet an unknown person whom we think we have perhaps seen once before, though we do not know where or when—or when, in a city new to us, we come upon a square, a street, a house, which we mysteriously seem to recognize... Böcklin also exploited the tragic aspects of statuary... created an entire world of his own, of a surprising lyricism, combining the preternaturalism of the Italian landscape with architectural elements.[14]

FRIEDRICH NIETZSCHE

A second vital experience of de Chirico's Munich years was his discovery of the prose of Friedrich Nietzsche. He read it avidly and there can be no doubt that its influence was profound and lasting. A quotation like the following, from Nietzsche's *Human, All Too Human*, must have clarified for the young Italian painter a longing, perhaps not wholly satisfied by Böcklin's art, for a supernatural intensity of expression. "Art," the German philosopher wrote, "is above all and first of all meant to embellish life, to make us to ourselves endurable... Hence art must conceal or transfigure everything that is ugly... A man who feels within himself a surplus of such powers of embellishment, concealment and transfiguration will finally seek to unburden himself of this surplus in works of art."[15]

Presumably de Chirico was especially impressed by Nietzsche's *The Birth of Tragedy*, and it is not difficult to imagine his poring over the words relating to the ideal artist—"and how now, through Apollonian dream-inspiration, his own state, i.e. his oneness with the primal source of the universe, reveals itself to him *in a symbolical dream-picture*."[16] And further: "The beauteous appearance of the dream worlds, in the production of which every man is a perfect artist, is the presupposition of all plastic art and in fact... of an important half of poetry also."[17] We have only to look at any one of de Chirico's early paintings to see that they propose a Nietzschean counter-reality based on reverie, incantation and dreams.

If Nietzsche's books supplied the general premise underlying the art of de Chirico's early career, they also helped suggest two of this art's principal subjects: the architectural squares of Italy; and the "metaphysical" still lifes (the third main category in de Chirico's early iconography has to do with mannequin figures, as we shall see). As to

27

the derivation of the Italian squares or "memories of Italy," the artist gives due credit to Nietzsche by describing in his autobiography what seems to him to have been the German philosopher's most remarkable innovation: "This innovation is a strange and profound poetry, infinitely mysterious and solitary, based on *Stimmung* (which might be translated . . . as atmosphere), based, I say, on the *Stimmung* of an autumn afternoon when the weather is clear and the shadows are longer than in summer, for the sun is beginning to be lower."[18] He adds: "the Italian city where this extraordinary phenomenon is most apparent is Turin"[19] (see illustrations, page 57). In this city Nietzsche spent his declining years and hailed it as "the only suitable place for me."[20] Moreover, as will appear, de Chirico visited Turin on his way to Paris in 1911, just before his mature series of Italian squares began. There is no reason to doubt that Nietzsche's prose played a key part in stimulating the painter's interest in creating a poetic reconstruction of the dream-lit piazzas of Italy.

Nietzsche's role in the evolution of de Chirico's "metaphysical" still lifes is equally important, if less precise. And here the philosopher's meaning for the young Italian artist was contrary to that of Böcklin. For whereas the latter for the most part relied on an intrinsic, mythological fantasy to give his pictures an aura of wonder, Nietzsche proposed a lyric reappraisal of everyday objects and scenes, suggesting an ulterior meaning beneath surface appearances. In *The Birth of Tragedy*, for example, he declares: "Indeed, the man of philosophic turn has a foreboding that underneath this reality in which we live and have our being, another and altogether different reality lies concealed, and that therefore it [the latter] is also an appearance; and Schopenhauer actually designates the gift of occasionally regarding men and things as mere phantoms and dream-pictures as the criterion of philosophical ability."[21] A glance at the illustrations of de Chirico's "metaphysical" still lifes (pages 219 and 236) should confirm their relationship to Nietzsche's theories.

OTHER GERMANIC INFLUENCES

Though Böcklin and Nietzsche were the paramount influences on the young de Chirico during his years in Munich, mention must also be made of the philosophers Schopenhauer and Otto Weininger, and of the artists Franz Stuck, Max Klinger and Alfred Kubin. As to the first-named, de Chirico wrote in an unpublished article of 1912, called "Meditations of a Painter" (Appendix B): "A truly immortal work of art can only be born through revelation. Schopenhauer has, perhaps, best defined and also (why not) explained such a moment when in *Parerga und Paralipomena* he says, 'To have original, extraordinary, and perhaps even immortal ideas, one has but to isolate oneself from the world for a few moments so completely that the most commonplace happenings appear to be new and unfamiliar, and in this way reveal their true essence.' If instead of the birth of *original, extraordinary, immortal* ideas, you imagine the birth of a work of art (painting or sculpture) in an artist's mind, you will have the principle of revelation in painting."[22] Moreover, it was Schopenhauer, as will appear in more detail, who was in good part responsible for de Chirico's interest in the phantomic aspects of statuary, and such celebrated essays as "On Apparitions" were of great importance in forming the philosophical climate of the painter's early period.

Otto Weininger's influence, though surely less basic, was nevertheless considerable and de Chirico at one point called the Austrian philosopher "the deepest psychologist I know about."[23] He added that Weininger's writings on esthetics are of decided help in appreciating Böcklin's art. As we shall see, they also have a direct bearing on certain of de Chirico's own pictures.

Returning to the subject of painters de Chirico admired in addition to Böcklin, perhaps mention should be made of Franz Stuck. But de Chirico himself has seldom referred to Stuck and there is no evidence that he ever admired the latter deeply. With Max Klinger the case is different. In an article published the year of that tormented artist's death (1920), de Chirico has told us what qualities he found most enviable in Klinger's work: "Feeling of sweet and Mediterranean serenity; vision of happy figures in the cool sunlight, lying on the beach in the shade of the pine trees... Inward consciousness of a distant yet not formidable horizon; yearning anxiety to recapture the calm that follows a climactic achievement."[24] In particular de Chirico liked, and indeed was to emulate, Klinger's ability to fuse contemporary reality with earlier temporal allusions—"However Klinger, psychologically more complex yet less classical than Böcklin, by combining in a single composition scenes of contemporary life and visions of antiquity, produces a highly troubling dream-reality."[25]

The specific works by Klinger that de Chirico preferred are also a matter of record. He liked certain paintings, especially the *Crucifixion, The Promenade, Prometheus* and the *Christ on Olympus;* he wrote enthusiastically of the German artist's strange sculptures in polychrome. Above all he revered the two series of prints, *Fantasy on Brahms* and *Paraphrase on the Finding of a Glove* (pages 22 and 23). In fact it seems reasonable to suppose that the latter series so impressed de Chirico that he included symbolic references to its central dramatic property—a glove—in certain pictures of his early career (pages 77, 196–198).

We know, moreover, that de Chirico's enthusiasm for Klinger did not fade with his youth. In the mid–1930s he completed a group of pictures of beach scenes with bathhouses. These pictures almost certainly owe something to Klinger's *Fantasy on Brahms* prints to which de Chirico referred in his 1920 article for *Il Convegno* as follows: "In order to make the poetic paradox of this scene more actual, Klinger places by the pianist a little wooden ladder which leads right into the water, like the steps of bathhouses at the beach. The invention of this ladder is delightfully ingenious. Reviewing my childhood memories, I still remember how alarmed and haunted I was by these seaside ladders."[26]

De Chirico's entire career shows many such reversions to the inspirations and memories of his early manhood and his childhood. Presumably their intervals of frequency will one day be determined accurately. Meanwhile it is interesting to note that he admired in Klinger a cinematic quality whose impact, if difficult to isolate, is often felt in de Chirico's own early work: "As I have already remarked, it possesses the dramatic quality of certain moving pictures in which the protagonists of tragedy and of modern life seem fixed in a fleeting, apparitional moment in a setting of extreme reality."[27]

` A prolific writer on art like many modern Italian painters, de Chirico has given us no article on Alfred Kubin to compare with his essays on Böcklin and Klinger. Yet Kubin's drawing of 1904–05, called *Vision of Italy* (page 23) is an astonishingly direct forerunner of de Chirico's series of pictures of Italian squares—a fact which struck the former artist forcefully some years ago, according to a letter addressed to the present writer.* It is obvious, however, that de Chirico's regard for Kubin, as for Franz Stuck, was much less pronounced than for Böcklin and Klinger. In much of Kubin's art an almost psychotic fantasy reigns; both he and Stuck often created images which are not enigmatic but unequivocally macabre or bizarre. We must remember that de Chirico himself has seldom if ever crossed into the territory of the fantastic-grotesque. Instead he has been the painter of what might be called a "jarred" reality in which chimerical allusions are restrained and held in careful, and therefore all the more disturbing, relationship to the plausible and the known. Even the powerfully fantastic *Disquieting Muses* of 1917 (page 135) uses as a setting a fairly exact replica of the Castello Estense in Ferrara (page 60), so that our credulity is not destroyed but upset. De Chirico seems to have avoided total fantasy for the simple reason that it could be too quickly rejected as such.

Quite apart from Böcklin and the German graphic artists just mentioned, it may be that de Chirico was exposed in Munich to the architectural projects of Schinkel, Weinbrenner and other figures of the Romantic era, including the great Frenchman, Ledoux. In fact the distinguished Italian art historian, Dr. C. L. Ragghianti, has suggested that the neo-classicism of these men may have led de Chirico to the use of dramatic, receding arcades, heavily shadowed, which occur so frequently in the latter's pictures of the early period.[28] However, an authority in such matters declares that the revival of interest in Schinkel, Weinbrenner and Ledoux did not take place in Germany until

* Alfred Kubin's letter to the writer, dated Oct. 22, 1950, reads in part as follows: "In answer to your question concerning my colored drawing, *Vision of Italy*, this sheet originated as early as 1904 or 1905, at a time when I was still entirely under the spell of my visions, which emerged in my consciousness from the lowest abysses ... I tried to establish firmly these apparitions ... When I saw some years ago in books and booklets illustrations of G. de Chirico's works, in many of them a similar mood struck me, with special reference to the *Vision of Italy*, but also in a few other of my sheets ... I lost track of the drawing, *Vision of Italy*; probably I sold it a long time ago."

many years after de Chirico had left Munich and painted (in Paris) his series of Italian squares.[29] Hence it seems more plausible to assume that Renaissance buildings and early nineteenth-century neo-classicism in de Chirico's native Italy were a more forceful architectural source. And nowhere in the painter's extensive writings on art is there any mention of the Northern neo-classicists of the Romantic period in architecture.

1909: THE RETURN TO ITALY

In 1909, "it was summer, I believe,"[30] de Chirico moved to Milan, where his brother had preceded him in the hope of having an opera produced. He lived in an apartment on the Via Petrarca and there, he says, "I painted Böcklinesque canvases."[31]

He did indeed, as even a casual glance at the illustrations on pages 19–21 will reveal. In these six paintings of 1909 there is little indication of the original style the artist was to develop in Paris after 1911. They are thoroughly Böcklinesque, and their romantic mythology was revived by the painter in 1922–23, during a period of renewed interest in Böcklin and, as previously noted, Dosso Dossi, with the result that some of his drawings of the latter time are sometimes mistakenly described as "pre-metaphysical." His early period (1910 to 1918) constitutes a quite separate entity within his art as a whole. If he has returned to its underlying inspiration at intervals, notably during the 1920s, he has done so in a new and different spirit.

Of the 1909 Milanese works here reproduced the writer has seen only one—*The Battle Between the Hoplites and the Centaurs*. Yet there is no reason whatever to doubt that the others are authentic pictures of the same year which the painter himself may have destroyed or repainted as he came to realize their over-dependence on Böcklin. Their existence, even in photographs, effectively disproves the 1908 date that appears on two works of the early Paris period—the *Self Portrait*, also known as *What shall I love if not the enigma?* (page 166) and *The Transformed Dream* (page 187). It is inconceivable that de Chirico could have executed these two paintings a year before the Böcklinesque canvases of 1909. Both pictures obviously belong to the artist's first Paris period (1911–15), and we shall discuss in due course the other contributory evidence that they were painted in 1911 and 1913 respectively.

FLORENCE, 1910

In 1910, suffering from the intestinal disorders which plagued his youth and perhaps had much to do with the melancholy temper of his early art, de Chirico moved to Florence. He remained more than a year, living with his mother when she was not away supervising his brother's musical career. At Florence, he declares, "I sometimes used to paint small pictures; my Böcklin period was over, and I was beginning to select subjects through which I attempted to express the intense, mysterious feeling I had discovered in Nietzsche: the melancholy of lovely autumn afternoons in Italian cities. This was a prelude to the Squares of Italy that I was to paint somewhat later in Paris."[32]

What specific pictures did de Chirico paint during his stay in Florence? Among them certainly was the portrait of his brother, Andrea (page 24). This picture is dated 1910 in Roman numerals, and in it the landscape, with its Böcklinesque centaur, seems closely related to the paintings completed at Milan in 1909. In addition to this engaging romantic work, it is probable that *The Enigma of an Autumn Afternoon* and *The Enigma of the Oracle* (page 165) were also finished at Florence in 1910. The first of the two is dated 1910; the second is said to be so dated, too, though it has disappeared and no completely legible photograph is available. De Chirico's inscribed dates are not, of course, always dependable. Yet very likely they are correct in these two instances, in which case de Chirico brought the pictures with him to Paris in 1911; they were both exhibited in the Salon d'Automne in 1912.

De Chirico would have had little else to exhibit in that Salon. We have his word that he produced almost nothing during his first year in the French capital—"I worked little, however; I painted few pictures."[33] Indeed soon after his arrival in Paris in July, 1911, his health became so poor that he was sent to Vichy for the cure and "I had not touched a brush or even a pencil for a long time."[34] And, finally, when a friend in Paris sent him to see the painter, Pierre Laprade, a member of the jury for the Salon d'Automne of 1912, de Chirico may well have taken along the two pictures he had finished at Florence in 1910, on the theory that works produced in Italy were more likely to be accepted than pictures by a newly recruited member of the School of Paris.

In any case *The Enigma of an Autumn Afternoon* and *The Enigma of the Oracle* are impressive works for an artist of twenty-two to have painted. The former picture, so the artist tells us, was "Inspired by the Piazza Santa Croce in Florence and contained the exceptional poetry I had discovered in Nietzsche's books . . ."[35] But by comparing an early twentieth-century photograph of the piazza (page 24) with de Chirico's painting of it, we can see how drastically the artist transformed his subject. Pazzi's mid-nineteenth century monument to Dante, standing in the middle of the actual piazza, has been converted into a mutilated classical figure whose Victorian origin is suggested primarily by the naturalistic tree trunk that supports it on its pedestal. The elaborate nineteenth-century façade of the fourteenth-century church of Santa Croce has been reduced to bare, arbitrary, structural essentials, as if the painter had stripped the church of its long accrual of ornament and envisioned it as a classical stage set. But de Chirico has retained the pilastered wall to the right of the church, including its tiled roof, and has even represented the diagonal abutment connecting the wall to Santa Croce. Behind the wall a train and the sails of a boat appear in place of Florentine architecture, and the scene is visible at the right through an imaginary portico. The revisions in actual source that de Chirico has made in *The Enigma of an Autumn Afternoon* may be taken as typical of the painter's procedure in creating his early series of Italian squares. Perhaps nowhere is his dual nostalgia for antiquity and for the Victorian era more apparent. This ambiguity of temporal inspiration, usually ignored by critics of the painter, will be discussed frequently throughout this book.

The figures in *The Enigma of an Autumn Afternoon* tend to qualify de Chirico's statement that, in Florence in 1910, "my Böcklin period was over."[36] For they are obviously still related to the figures of Böcklin. Yet the picture must be regarded as a key work in the evolution of one kind of twentieth-century art. Its composition is horizontal, but at one point the eye of the observer is led far back to the horizon, with its paradoxical juxtaposition of boat and train. The long shadows in the foreground strengthen the illusion of deep space, and the portico at the right is placed at an angle to the piazza, facing the luminous distance. Here clearly (and probably for the first time) is prefigured the artist's preoccupation with perspective as a poetic-philosophical instrument, a preoccupation which led de Chirico years later to write: "Who can deny the troubling connection that exists between perspective and metaphysics?"[37] Thus by 1910 the Italian painter had begun to revive for its emotive value a spatial emphasis which the artists of the Renaissance had treasured primarily as an aid to greater realism. We shall see presently how contrary was de Chirico's manipulation of space to that of nearly all his elders and contemporaries in the School of Paris. *The Enigma of an Autumn Afternoon* is a prophetic picture, though it has the tremble of new authority.

The Enigma of the Oracle, despite its left section's patent debt to Böcklin, is an even more original work. It is less picturesque than the *Autumn Afternoon*, to begin with, and it illustrates more clearly the purification of Böcklin's romanticism that de Chirico instinctively undertook. For whereas Böcklin's excessively literary inspiration often led him in the direction of saccharine rusticism or overt melodrama, his successor's art is tempered and cleansed. De Chirico's vision is not so much mythological as mythopoeic; for Böcklin's creaky theatrics it substitutes a subtle legerdemain.

The disturbing white head which appears behind the curtain in *The Enigma of the Oracle* contributes to an atmosphere of malaise which cannot be shaken off and which is not alleviated by the artist's statement that the picture is concerned with "a lyricism of Greek prehistory."[38] What is the figure behind the curtain doing? What manner of dream image is it? Such questions could scarcely be asked about Böcklin's figures, for in matters of iconography the Swiss painter was usually explicit to the point of banality. But in relation to de Chirico's early art as a whole, they are questions that suggest themselves time and again. And if the *Oracle* lacks the impact of inevitability which is so strong in slightly later works, it nevertheless conveys the impression of uneasy suspense to which the painter has referred in one of his prose poems: "Late in the afternoon, when the evening light was beginning slowly to obscure the mountains to the east of the city, and when the cliffs beneath the citadel were turning mauve, one could feel that SOMETHING WAS GATHERING, as the nurses would say while gossiping on the benches of the public square . . ."[39]

The Autumn Afternoon and the Oracle prefigure what a modern painter-critic, Gordon Onslow-Ford, has described in lectures as "Chirico City,"—a vista of silent squares, peopled by shadows and statues, bounded by distant horizons and marked by an elegiac beauty and vast dignity. If the basic inspiration for these pictures came from Florence, ancient Greece and Nietzsche's prose, the world they celebrate is a dream world through which, in his imagination, de Chirico traveled in an "old-fashioned locomotive chugging forward along a cliff overhanging the sea."[40] The young Italian painter had come upon a romantic territory which many artists before him had explored. But he had also found a personal way to describe this territory in terms of a strange and memorable foreboding, to portray it as alive but haunted, to hold it quiet but breathing. A number of earlier painters had used the same dramatic properties—old architecture, curtained doorways, distant horizons, mourning figures in a failing light. Perhaps none had managed to transpose these properties so evocatively from everyday reality to dream, to create so striking an imagery of counterlogic.

The painter himself, in an unpublished article of 1912, has given us an especially clear account of how this counterlogic functioned as an inspirational force:

...let me recount how I had the revelation of a picture that I will show this year at the Salon d'Automne, entitled Enigma of an Autumn Afternoon. One clear autumnal afternoon I was sitting on a bench in the middle of the Piazza Santa Croce in Florence. It was of course not the first time I had seen this square. I had just come out of a long and painful intestinal illness, and I was in a nearly morbid state of sensitivity. The whole world, down to the marble of the buildings and the fountains seemed to me to be convalescent. In the middle of the square rises a statue of Dante draped in a long cloak, holding his works clasped against his body, his laurel-crowned head bent thoughtfully earthward. The statue is in white marble, but time has given it a gray cast, very agreeable to the eye. The autumn sun, warm and unloving, lit the statue and the church façade. Then I had the strange impression that I was looking at all these things for the first time, and the composition of my picture came to my mind's eye. Now each time I look at this painting I again see that moment. Nevertheless the moment is an enigma to me, for it is inexplicable. And I like also to call the work which sprang from it an enigma.[41]

THE TRIP TO PARIS: TURIN, 1911

In 1911, stirred by the letters of his brother, who had moved to Paris, de Chirico decided to join Andrea in the French capital. He had been suffering, as noted in his manuscript above, from a nervous disorder which he describes as "almost an extreme crisis of melancholy."[42] His brother's reports on Paris' extraordinary pre-war activity in the arts must have appealed to him strongly at the time, though he now dismisses this

34

activity as illusory: "Later I came to realize that all this exists only in men's fancy and that people are no more intelligent in Paris than they are in Rome, London, Madrid, Berlin or Pernambuco."[43]

The painter left Florence with his mother in July, 1911. On their way north to France, the two stopped for several days at Turin, a city to which de Chirico was probably attracted because of Nietzsche's identification with it. At any rate the Piedmont capital made a vital impression on the young artist and became, with Florence, a point of departure for his series of paintings of Italian squares.

De Chirico's enthusiasm for Turin is understandable, for that city is surely one of the most curious and unforgettable in all Europe. Its arcades (a favorite motif in the painter's early art) are so extensive that a local author has written a book tracing a full day's walk which may be taken without once leaving their protective shade. Turin's architecture, dominated by Alessandro Antonelli's fantastic Mole Antonelliana, begun in 1864 and rising 165 metres in the air until recently damaged by a storm, covers a wide range of styles from medieval to late Victorian, with notable and grandiose examples of late eighteenth- and early nineteenth-century neo-classicism. In particular de Chirico must have been fascinated by Turin's vast, mournful piazzas (page 57) and by the lingering vestiges of its brief glory as center of the United Italian Kingdom under Cavour and under Victor Emmanuel II of whom Nietzsche, in his final madness, thought himself the reincarnation.

In no other Italian city is the nineteenth century so aggressively preserved and we should remember, as mentioned in connection with *The Enigma of an Autumn Afternoon*, that de Chirico's early paintings often achieve an odd amalgam of Renaissance and Victorian properties and atmosphere. Certainly the young artist must have looked hard at Carlo Marocchetti's nineteenth-century equestrian monuments (page 58) for, as we shall see in greater detail, one of these sculptures, imaginatively re-created in silhouette, haunts the quiet distances in several pictures of his early career (pages 170 and 190).

Apart from Marocchetti's monumental works there are to be found in Turin a number of sculptures of standing, frock-coated figures erected as memorials to illustrious citizens of Piedmont (page 59). De Chirico's use of these sculptural models will be discussed at greater length in relation to the pictures in which they appear (pages 182, 189). But we may note in passing that such sculptures seem unusually ghostly in Turin, partly because of the frequency with which they occur. And there can be no doubt that they confirmed the painter in his respect for Schopenhauer's theories on the apparitional aspects of public sculptures. In 1919 de Chirico wrote: "Schopenhauer advised his fellow countrymen not to place the statues of their famous men on high columns or on pedestals, but on low plinths, 'as they do in Italy, where some marble men seem to be on a level with the passers-by and seem to walk beside them.'"[44]

From Turin de Chirico and his mother proceeded to Paris, arriving on July 14, 1911 and stopping in a hotel before moving to an apartment. The painter's intestinal disorders grew steadily worse and, as noted, he was forced to spend several weeks in Vichy taking a cure. His health improved gradually, but there is no reason to doubt his statement (see page 32) that he did little work. His quite prolific early career in Paris did not really begin until the autumn of 1912, and the often repeated claim that his art matured abruptly after his arrival in the French capital is false. The claim is usually based on the fact that one of his most celebrated pictures, *The Nostalgia of the Infinite* (page 53), bears the inscribed date 1911. But this date is incorrect, as the present writer has pointed out elsewhere,[45] for reasons which will be expanded in discussing the series of paintings to which the *Nostalgia* properly belongs (page 51).

There are, however, a few pictures which were almost certainly completed during the artist's first year and a half in Paris. Among them are two self portraits in profile (page 166). The first of these (possibly begun in Florence in 1910), with its inscription "What shall I love if not the enigma?," is dated 1908. This date is false and a macrophotograph of the picture's signature and date, taken soon after the canvas was cleaned in 1950, reveals that the digits "08" have been superimposed over underlying digits "11." (See page 126).

Superimposed by whom, and when, and why? None of these questions has yet been answered authoritatively. Yet it seems possible that de Chirico himself may have affixed the 1908 date at some point, as he may also have done in the case of *The Transformed Dream*, a work actually executed in 1913 (page 187). There would have been no plausible reason for a forger to alter the date of the self portrait (or of *The Transformed Dream*). The picture remained in France until it was brought to New York after 1933. And since Parisian interest in de Chirico's early period centered, from roughly 1926 onward, on works executed between 1910 and the end of 1917, there would have been little incentive for a forger to change the date. To inscribe the painting as 1908 might have established it as an immature student work, completed when the artist was still a student at the Munich Academy.

There are, however, two possible reasons why de Chirico himself might have altered the self portrait's date (and also that of *The Transformed Dream*) quite apart from any possible lapse of memory. Around 1919, as we shall see in detail, he began to be irritated by the share of credit given Carlo Carrà for the achievements of the *scuola metafisica* at Ferrara (1915–18) of which he and Carrà were the founders. Since Carrà was older than he and by 1910 had attracted attention as one of the five original Futurist artists, de Chirico may have wished to assert his own greater precocity by claiming that he was already producing mature works as early as 1908. Yet since the self portrait remained in France until 1933, the artist himself could not have altered its date until after his return to Paris in 1925 (he was in Italy from 1915 until 1925). By that time, however, his rivalry with Carrà was no longer a pressing matter. Soon after he moved to Paris for the second time, his attention was diverted from the Italian art scene by his bitter quarrel with the surrealists.

A summary of this quarrel, so important for de Chirico's evolution as a painter, will be given in due course. But we may note here that by March, 1926, the surrealists had begun to repudiate de Chirico's post-war return to classicism. Simultaneously they had commenced to make precise their own estimate of his art's creative duration—from 1911 through 1917. It is not difficult to imagine the enraged de Chirico deciding that he would prove them as ill-informed in dating the first flowering of his genius as in dating its demise.

At any rate the 1908 date is certainly wrong for the self portrait, as it is for *The Transformed Dream*. When we remember the Böcklinesque compositions executed at Milan in 1909, it seems inconceivable that the self portrait could have been completed a year before. The latter picture is more assured than the portrait of de Chirico's brother which we know was completed in Florence in 1910. If it still owes something to Böcklin and perhaps also to Franz Stuck, it is nevertheless much more than a student's exercise. It announces the great Paris series of 1912 to 1915; its right date, in the writer's opinion, is 1911.

A similar, if less complicated, problem of dating arises in connection with the second early self portrait in profile (page 166). This portrait is now signed and dated 1911 at the base of its tower. But as reproduced in Vitrac's monograph of 1927, the composition includes a foreground border, since removed, on which the original signature and a date that appears to be 1912 are visible. Perhaps it was this self portrait which de Chirico sent to the Salon d'Automne of 1912. It is any case a later work than the 1911 self portrait bearing the inscription "What shall I love if not the enigma?" discussed above. It shows the painter as older and leaner, perhaps as a result of his illness in France. Moreover, in it are included iconographical elements characteristic of his more settled Parisian style—a tower with blowing pennants, a brick wall, geometric and arbitrary forms.*

---

* A contemporary critic has suggested that de Chirico was led to the juxtaposition of human and geometric forms, as in the second self portrait, by the example of the seventeenth-century Bolognese artist, Domenichino.[46] But the chiaroscuro of de Chirico's self portrait, if stemming obliquely from the Baroque tradition, is dominated by a linear modeling which harks back to fifteenth-century precedent, and it is such masters as Antonello da Messina and Botticelli who come to mind. Furthermore, we know that de Chirico was contemptuous of native Baroque painting throughout his early career (an ironical fact in view of his recent works!). In 1921 he published in *Valori Plastici* an article entitled "La Mania del Seicento," in which he declared: "The seventeenth century is a prelude to the decadence of today's painting. It is with the artists of that period that the flame of revelation and

The second self portrait's heavy contours and parallel cross-hatchings are again used in the *Nude* (page 167) which, though not dated, must have been completed during the same year and a half (1911–12) and is quite probably the picture de Chirico exhibited in the Salon d'Automne of 1913 as *Etude*. Its almost academic though unusually ruthless realism is tempered, as in the case of the self portrait, by the strange structure to the right of the figure. Here de Chirico substitutes for sixteenth-century Mannerist portraiture's specific architectural references, an enigmatic building of no recognizable epoch or style. If the *Nude* is the sort of studio piece the new arrival in Paris might have been expected to undertake, its setting announces the painter's idiosyncrasy of vision. The building's arbitrary perspective foretells the headlong extensions of space that were soon to follow in de Chirico's art; its yawning, cavernous apertures remind us of the painter's later tribute to Giotto: "In Giotto, too, the use of architecture is highly metaphysical. All the openings—doors, arches, windows—while closely related to the figures, induce a foreboding of cosmic mystery."[48]

Obviously de Chirico was moving steadily in the direction of an art of dreamed sensation, following Nietzsche's dictum that the artist must refute reality without scruple. And Germanic sources were still important to him. *Morning Meditation* (opposite), dated 1912 and properly so, reveals that Böcklin's example was not yet lost to sight. The picture's warm tan and blue tonality makes clear that de Chirico had not yet definitely settled on the hard, lean yet luminous palette which was to distinguish his great pictures of 1913 and 1914. This painting could not conceivably have been executed a year later than *The Nostalgia of the Infinite*, a fact which adds considerable weight to the contention that the true date of the *Nostalgia* is 1913 or 1914, not 1911.

DE CHIRICO AND THE SCHOOL OF PARIS

It is perhaps time to pause for a moment to consider the artistic climate of Paris in which de Chirico was now, toward the end of 1912, beginning to work. Referring to his early career in the French city, the painter has said: ... "what I did was absolutely different from what was being done at that time in Paris..."[49] It was indeed. In 1912–13 the most influential advanced movement in Parisian art was, of course, cubism, about to enter its "synthetic" phase. By then cubism had been supplemented by the total abstractions of Kandinsky and others. The cubists and the "pure" abstractionists

discovery becomes extinguished"...[47] In the same article de Chirico praises by comparison such earlier masters as Fra Angelico, Carpaccio, Signorelli, Botticelli and Piero della Francesca. And while the art of these masters is perhaps more directly related to de Chirico's neo-classicism of the early 1920s than to the proto-surrealism of his first Paris period, the impact of the Renaissance is evident in his self portrait of 1912. De Chirico could not have failed to be impressed by the masterworks of the fifteenth century during his year in Florence. In Paris he probably looked at the Louvre's pictures of the *quattrocento* with the quickened sensibility of exile.

Morning Meditation, 1912. 20½ x 28″. Collection Riccardo Jucker, Milan

were allied in a common goal—to overthrow the tyranny of literary, historical and realistic subject matter, to renew from within the structure and meaning of art. With the significant exception of de Chirico's countrymen, the Futurists, most of the adherents of the abstract revolt were agreed that painting must abandon the expository preoccupations of earlier artists and assert its autonomy as esthetic experience.

In general insurrectionary premise the young de Chirico was on the side of the cubists and their direct followers in the School of Paris, though there is no reason to doubt his claim that he became aware of their program only gradually after he moved to France.[50] There are, however, crucial differences between his approach to art and theirs. For example, whereas the cubists were most of all interested in the architecture of painting itself, de Chirico throughout a good part of his early Parisian career was devoted to the painting of architecture. "Architecture complements nature," he later wrote. "This marked an advance in man's understanding of metaphysical discoveries."[51]

It is no accident, of course, that de Chirico has repeatedly expressed his admiration for Poussin and Claude—two artists for whom the lyric and associational virtues of architecture were a consuming passion.* The cubists, on the contrary, though impressed by Poussin's principles of abstract design, were largely indifferent to the romanticism of buildings, old or modern. We cannot imagine Picasso, Braque, Léger or Gris writing about architecture as de Chirico was to write: "In the planning of cities, in the architecture of houses, squares, gardens, promenades, seaports, railway-stations—are the very foundations of a great metaphysical esthetic. The Greeks were most scrupulous about such buildings because they were guided by their esthetic or philosophical attitude: the porches, the shady walks, the terraces theatrically extended so as to afford the best view of the great spectacles of nature (Homer, Aeschylus); the tragedy of serenity."[52]

In trying to recover the architectonic truths of painting itself, the cubists and their followers used geometric forms, among them Cézanne's famous "the cylinder, the sphere, the cone." Throughout his early career de Chirico, too, was devoted to these forms, but his attitude toward them was different from that of the abstractionists. As an enthusiast for Otto Weininger's writings, he eagerly accepted the German philosopher's rather mystical concept of geometry's emotive power.

The arch, for instance, is one of the most persistent elements in de Chirico's youthful vision. In explaining its fascination for him he quoted Weininger as follows: "The arc of the circle, as an ornament, may be beautiful: it does not signify perfect completeness, beyond all criticism, as does Midgard's snake that encircles the world. In the arc there is still something unaccomplished which needs to be and can be completed: *it still permits presentiment* ..."[53]

---

* De Chirico's enthusiastic opinion of Poussin and Claude is expressed in his two articles in *Valori Plastici*, "Sull'arte metafisica" and "Il senso architettonico nella pittura antica."

The artist goes on in the same article to give his own views on the metaphysical interpretation of triangles and squares, but these will be mentioned in connection with his still lifes of a slightly later date. For now let us simply note that de Chirico regarded geometric forms as symbolic, whereas to most advanced painters in the Paris of 1912–13 such forms were the materials of a new and firmer pictorial construction.

An even more fundamental divergence between de Chirico's program and that of the leaders of the School of Paris lay in their separate means of suggesting space. The latter, following in post-impressionism's wake, were nearly all accepting with frankness and pride the two-dimensional limitations of the painter's canvas. To the fauves, the cubists and the Central European expressionists, it seemed dishonest to try to give the illusion of a dominant third dimension which did not exist in fact within the flat, painted surface. To attempt to do so through linear manipulation was for many of these artists an especially odious heresy. They remembered—and cherished—Cézanne's dictum: "I try to render perspective solely by means of color." But de Chirico, and he almost alone in avant-garde circles, was determined to revive the deep perspective of humanism, not for reasons of plausibility or scientific accuracy, as with the mid-fifteenth-century Italians, but as an instrument of poetic and philosophical suggestion. And for him line was of supreme importance in defining space, as it had been for his Renaissance predecessors.

Not until after World War I, by which date de Chirico had consciously begun his return to classicism, did the painter make his view in this matter of linear perspective wholly clear. Yet there can be little doubt that his article, "Classicismo Pittorico," published in *La Ronda* in 1920, listed precepts in which he had believed much earlier. "Therefore we can assert," he wrote, "that like Ingres and the Italians of the fifteenth century, the painters of ancient Greece believed that drawing and drawing alone was the foundation of truly great art. In the mystique of line which characterizes all truly classical art, we can perceive an aversion for the aggregation of useless masses, for the solid fleshiness which is alien to all spiritual subtlety."[54]

In short de Chirico proposed as early as 1912–13 to recapture through predominantly linear methods an illusory atmosphere of infinity, wherein architecture, figures, objects and statuary would appear utterly detached from a near and present reality. "Who can deny," he was later to write, "the troubling connection between perspective and metaphysics?"[55]

De Chirico and the members of the cubist-abstract group, despite their differences in aim and procedure, were obviously both opposed to realism as the nineteenth century had come to understand it. He (as much as they) was contemptuous of impressionism's devotion to surface appearances. In 1919 he wrote: "Spiritual impotence leads to naturalism and fatally reduces painting to a slapdash negligence toward the work of art which thereupon ceases to count as a precious object, a marvel, a miracle, and is lowered to a level of a mere artifice, more or less original, more or less qualified to satisfy the demands of connoisseurs of laundry and kitchen painting."[56]

In place of the work of art as a more or less faithful reflection of existing reality, de Chirico intended to create an imagery of incantation and revelation. And like the cubists he understood that to do so required a violent break with the art of the past. In 1913 he wrote down his own ultimatum against the accepted canons of realism in painting: "What is needed above all," he said, "is to rid art of all that has been its familiar content until now; all subject, all idea, all thought, all symbol must be put aside ... Thought must so detach itself from all usual logic and sense, must so remove itself from all human fetters that all things appear to it anew—as if lit for the first time by a brilliant star."[57]

The last clause in this quotation gives us another clue to the nature of de Chirico's deviation from the theories of the cubists. For while the cubists and their associates wished to rebuild the visible world from what they considered to be sounder materials, de Chirico wanted to *relight* the painter's world, to restore a sense of the uncanny in suggesting scenes and objects, to give art the bright and disturbing clarity "of the dream and of the child mind."[58] In this aim, he was, of course, a vital forerunner of the entire surrealist movement.

De Chirico also made clear that in his attempt to relight painting, he intended to use only artificial sources of illumination. He was in full reaction against the impressionists, particularly as to their use of daylight in as empirical, i. e. "true," a manner as their research would allow.

What impressionism should be [he wrote in 1913]: A building, a garden, a statue, a person — each makes an *impression* upon us. The problem is to reproduce this impression in the most faithful possible fashion. Several painters have been called impressionists who at bottom were not. In my opinion there is no point in using technical means (divisionism, pointillism, etc.) to try to give the illusion of what we call truth. For example, to paint a sunlit landscape trying in every way to give the sensation of light. Why? I too see the light; however well it may be reproduced, I also see it in nature, and a painting that has this for its purpose will never be able to give me the sensation of something new, of something that, previously, *I have not known*. While if a man faithfully reproduces the strange sensations that he feels, this can always give new joys to any sensitive and intelligent person.[59]

A final basic difference between de Chirico's purpose and that of the cubists is conveyed by the concluding sentence in this quotation. For while Georges Braque, for example, by 1917 was professing his faith in the intelligence that controls emotion, de Chirico was hailing the emotion that controls intelligence and was planning to transfigure reality in order to supply it with an emotive as opposed to a formal validity. To repeat, in place of the cubists' painstaking reconstruction of the visible world from its plastic components, the young Italian artist wished to make a new world appear as though by hallucination—or not at all.

42

At the Salon des Indépendants of 1913, de Chirico was represented by three paintings: *The Enigma of the Hour, The Melancholy of Departure* and *The Enigma of Arrival and of the Afternoon.* Since the Salon opened very early in the year, all three pictures were probably completed in 1912. But only one of them can be identified with certainty: *The Enigma of the Hour* (page 168). This picture is an imaginative reconstruction of a fifteenth-century Florentine courtyard in the manner of Brunelleschi; its closest model in existing architecture would seem to be the court adjoining the Brancacci chapel in Santa Maria del Carmine (page 58), whose round fountain de Chirico may have converted into a flat oblong, while retaining the gallery with tiled roof. In any case, *The Enigma of the Hour* marks the beginning of de Chirico's use of architecture as a predominant iconographical theme. Its foreground figure, however, still recalls Böcklin's *Odysseus.* And the picture's color is rather bland and sweet, as in the *Morning Meditation* of 1912. Obviously *The Enigma of the Hour* is not a work of 1914, under which date it has often been published, for the artist permanently abandoned a soft, Böcklinesque tonality sometime in 1913.

Both *Morning Meditation* and *The Enigma of the Hour* are images presented in profile, so to speak, and their spatial arrangement is shallow and horizontal. But late in 1912 (or possibly early in 1913) de Chirico turned to a revival of the Renaissance's deep linear perspective, already briefly discussed. The new spatial exaggeration occurs, perhaps for the first time, in *Melancholy* (page 169)* a work that could be the picture shown in the 1913 Salon des Indépendants as *The Melancholy of Departure,* though the latter title has been used indiscriminately by critics for a number of early de Chiricos which certainly did not bear this title originally. The deepened perspective occurs, however, mainly in the left section of the composition, where an egress from the courtyard leads past silhouetted figures to a far landscape. The illusion of endless

---

* Another version of *Melancholy* (page 146) was published in *Les feuilles libres* for May-June, 1926, as *Souvenir d'Italie.* It differs from the Watson painting (page 169) in important respects: it lacks the lettering "Melanconia" on the statue's pedestal; it is signed in de Chirico's slanting handwriting and bears no date, whereas the Watson version is dated 1912 and signed in the artist's early, vertical style. The definition of the shadows is not identical in both pictures, nor is the painting of the architecture, and the draperies of Ariadne are tighter in handling in the Rothschild version and are arranged differently as they fall over the pedestal.

The writer has never seen the Watson picture, but had always believed it much earlier in date than the other version. Recently, however, the latter painting was examined in excellent light in the American collection to which it now belongs, whereas previously it had been studied in poor light in the apartment of M. Marcel Raval in Paris. The writer's conclusion is that the Rothschild picture was painted not later than 1914; its golden tonality and thinness of pigment suggest a comparison with *Mystery and Melancholy of a Street* (page 73), known to have been painted in 1914. M. Raval acquired the Rothschild picture around 1920 — some years before de Chirico began to make later copies of his own early works.

distance is heightened by the abrupt scaling-down of these shadowy figures in relation to the large foreground statue of Ariadne—an iconographical motif here first utilized and soon to appear in a fairly extensive series of paintings by de Chirico (see pages 174–180). The picture's depth is still further increased by long shadows cast by figures, a statue and architecture. These shadows are not yet as arbitrary and geometric as they will become in slightly later works by the painter. But they are already dramatized to an unnatural degree. Often, as in the foreground shadow cast by an unseen figure or sculpture, they are used for phantomic effect.

One more picture dated 1912 deserves mention here. This is *The Lassitude of the Infinite* (page 175). But in this work the break with the relative realism of the other pictures of 1912 is so extreme that quite likely the canvas was finished in 1913. The geometric simplification of the shadows, plus the picture's strange format, hint at a slightly later date than that inscribed on the canvas itself.

FRIENDSHIPS IN PARIS; GUILLAUME APOLLINAIRE

In view of de Chirico's isolation from advanced developments in the art of pre-war Paris, it is the more remarkable that he so soon attracted the attention of a small but influential group of artists and writers. Through a Greek friend he had met the painter, Pierre Laprade, on whose recommendation *The Enigma of the Oracle* and *The Enigma of an Autumn Afternoon* (both probably painted in Florence in 1910), plus the self portrait, had been accepted by the Salon d'Automne of 1912. None of the three pictures was sold and, according to the artist, the first of his works to be purchased was *The Rose Tower* (page 170) bought from the Salon d'Automne of 1913 by Oliver Senn. But de Chirico's pictures were apparently noticed, if not unreservedly admired, by several critics.

Among these critics may have been the most important of all for that pre-war period—Guillaume Apollinaire. At any rate, in 1913 de Chirico began to attend Apollinaire's "Sundays" at 202bis Boulevard Saint-Germain, where the poet took an apartment in the autumn and where he lived until his departure for the war in December, 1914. (Apollinaire returned to the apartment when invalided out of the French army, and his widow has kept it, nearly intact, since his death in 1918.) During the years 1913 and 1914, some of de Chirico's paintings were acquired by the poet, then the most effective champion of avant-garde movements in Parisian art. In describing the famous apartment on the Boulevard Saint-Germain, Philippe Soupault has written: "There were very beautiful Picassos, a Marie Laurencin and an impressive de Chirico of the good period in the bedroom—the handsomest room in the apartment."[60]

According to a letter received from Apollinaire's widow,[61] there were actually three de Chirico paintings in the poet's apartment during the last years of his life. One of these was destroyed by the Germans during the Occupation; a second picture, seemingly impossible to trace, was sold by Mme Apollinaire. The third painting, still at 202bis Boulevard Saint-Germain, is the famous oil portrait of Apollinaire, completed in 1914 (page 201). A drawing for the portrait also exists (page 64). For stylistic reasons it seems possible that this is a later work, perhaps undertaken at the instigation of the surrealists after de Chirico's return to Paris in 1925. The artist's drawings of 1912–15, judging by known authentic examples (pages 81–85), are sketchy in execution and were probably intended as working notes rather than finished works, whereas the portrait-drawing of Apollinaire is intricately modeled, suggesting the more finished technique of de Chirico's later career. Yet we must keep in mind the fact that either the oil portrait or the drawing was presently transcribed into a wood engraving by Pierre Roy, to be used as the frontispiece for an unpublished edition of Apollinaire's *Calligrammes* (page 64). With publication of his image in mind, de Chirico may have taken special care in preparing his drawing of the poet and may have completed it in 1914, before or soon after the oil painting was done.

In the painting, the drawing, and the woodcut, Apollinaire's strong profile appears as a silhouette in the background. On his head there is a white circular outline startlingly similar to that formed by the bandages he was obliged to wear after a trepanation for a serious (and eventually fatal) head injury received in combat in March, 1916 (page 64). The charcoal drawing for the portrait shows the poet's head pierced by a small hole, a fact which the surrealists in particular have described as a prophetic reference to Apollinaire's wound from a fragment of artillery shell. If the drawing was completed some time *after* the poet's death, this additional evidence of de Chirico's prophetic powers must be rejected. But even without it, the case for the portrait-image's sense of augury remains impressive. And what is especially curious is that Apollinaire himself twice referred to the picture as "my portrait as human target" in letters written in May, 1915, ten months before he was wounded.*

In 1913 and 1914 Apollinaire was the principal literary champion of cubism and subsidiary trends toward abstract art. His recognition of the young Italian painter's solitary and curious genius is therefore all the more remarkable. Certainly it was the decisive factor in de Chirico's rise to fame, for praise or even mention by the poet was an enormous asset to any rising young artist. In reviewing the Salon d'Automne of 1913,

---

* On May 6, 1915, Apollinaire wrote to de Chirico's dealer, Paul Guillaume: "I would be grateful if you would ask G. de Chirico to take or have sent to my janitor, who will put it in my apartment, my portrait *en homme-cible*."

On May 16, 1915, he again wrote Guillaume: "I would have preferred that *L'homme-cible* was at my house, where my mother could have looked at it when she felt like it, since in addition to being a singular and profound work of art, it is also a good likeness as a portrait—a shadow or rather a silhouette such as people made at the beginning of the nineteenth century."

Both letters were published in *Les Arts à Paris* for Jan. 7, 1923.

Apollinaire declared: "I must also mention a few additional works . . . the metaphysical landscapes of M. de Chirico."[62] The following March, in discussing the Salon des Indépendants, he wrote: "The strangeness of the plastic enigmas proposed by M. de Chirico still escapes most people. To describe the fatal character of contemporary things, the painter uses that most modern recourse—surprise."[63]

The concept of "surprise" as a vital ingredient in a new esthetic of literature and art was a central part of Apollinaire's premise, as he himself repeatedly made clear— "The new spirit resides equally in surprise. It is that about it which is most alive and new. Surprise is the great new means."[64] And this concept unquestionably had a great effect on de Chirico's aims as a painter. Indeed Roger Shattuck's words about Apollinaire's poetry apply closely to de Chirico's early paintings in general: "Apollinaire's particular technique of distortion has already been discussed: the animation of dead objects, the defiance of time and place, the most rash and distant of associations, and the gratuitous combination of things in order to produce unforeseen meanings. The usual logic both of reason and of our feelings is put aside in order to find the value of paradox insisted upon so tenaciously that it becomes a simple, positive fact."[65]

If Apollinaire was de Chirico's first powerful supporter, there is some evidence that he was not always solemnly convinced by the latter's pictures. At least an intimate friend of the poet has reported: "Apollinaire burst out laughing when he looked at them, but he always refused to concede to me that these works of a hypochondriacal dislocation had no purely artistic merit."[66] Yet there can be no doubt that the poet's regard for the young painter deepened steadily. The two men saw each other frequently, so frequently in fact that the legend has arisen, chiefly through the surrealists' urging, that de Chirico's pictures were given their provocative titles by Apollinaire as soon as they were completed. There is little evidence to support the legend. To begin with, the painter himself had begun to use such titles several years before he met Apollinaire, notably in the cases of *The Enigma of an Autumn Afternoon* and *The Enigma of the Oracle*. Moreover, de Chirico has always shown decided literary gifts; his astonishing novel *Hebdomeros* (1929), would in itself be adequate proof of his ability to invent his own titles. And finally, some of these titles occur in the pages of an unpublished manuscript written by de Chirico before the First World War (Appendix B). Among these titles is *The Enigma of Fatality*, a title which André Breton once assured the writer could have been devised only by Guillaume Apollinaire. There is, in short, no tenable reason to suppose that any of the authentic titles of de Chirico's early pictures were invented by anyone but himself. And these titles were applied, we should remember, at a time when nearly all the advanced painters of Europe were insisting on the simplest and least "literary" descriptions for their pictures, though gradually the Dadaists and such independent pioneers as Paul Klee brought longer titles—either explanatory or provocative—back into favor.

46

It was probably Apollinaire who called de Chirico's art to Picasso's attention. The Spanish master seems to have been impressed, though his only recorded comment is his description of his Italian colleague, seven years his junior, as "a painter of railroad stations."[67] The phrase seems odd in view of the fact that only one of de Chirico's early paintings—the *Gare Montparnasse* of 1914 (page 191)—specifically depicts a railroad station. Yet these paintings as a group are often concerned with trains and the moods of travel. Moreover, several of de Chirico's "Italian squares" suggest by allusion the bleak expanses and long corridors of railway terminals—an impression heightened by the frequent inclusion of clocks and ramps. Indeed, de Chirico's early pictures sometimes propose a curious cross-reference between high classical architecture and its modern derivatives in railroad-station engineering, a point which will be developed later on in these pages. Picasso's description of his Italian colleague is therefore understandable. His interest in the youthful de Chirico seems to have survived the years in that he acquired from his great friend, the late Paul Eluard, the manuscript here published as Appendix A. And in pre-war Paris Picasso's esteem, together with that of Apollinaire, Max Jacob, Maurice Raynal and other eminent personalities, made it possible in 1913 for de Chirico to secure a dealer (Paul Guillaume) and to begin his professional career in earnest.

THE YOUNG DE CHIRICO'S REPUTATION IN ITALY

In his native Italy de Chirico continued to be relatively unknown until after the First World War, though mention must surely be made of the one effective champion his art attracted at an earlier date. This was the painter-critic, Ardengo Soffici, who had gone to Paris at the turn of the century, remained for seven or eight years and returned to Italy to collaborate with Giovanni Papini in editing the important Futurist magazine, *Lacerba* (1913–15). Considering Soffici's abstract predilections in art, his regard for the youthful de Chirico was as remarkable as that of Apollinaire. Apollinaire seems to have been well aware of this fact, for in *Paris-Journal* for July 14, 1914, he printed in his column, "Les Arts; Nouveaux peintres," a long and eloquent quotation on de Chirico's art published by Soffici in *Lacerba*, July 1, 1914. Soffici wrote as follows:

Imagine a painter who, in the inflamed center of ceaseless and more hazardous researches... continues to paint with the calm application of a solitary old master, a sort of Paolo Uccello in love with his divine perspective and insensible of everything apart from his beautiful geometry. I have written the name of Paolo Uccello without any intention of establishing an essential resemblance.

G. de Chirico is above all absolutely modern, and if geometry and the effects of perspective are the primordial elements of his art, his usual means of expressing emotion, it is also true that his work does not resemble that of any other, old or modern, created from these elements. The painting of de Chirico is not painting in the sense that the word is used today.

47

One could define it as a dream writing. By means of almost infinite escapes—of arcades and façades, of bold straight lines, of looming masses of simple colors, of almost funereal lights and shadows—he ends in fact by expressing this sense of vastness, solitude, immobility and ecstasy which sometimes is produced in our souls by certain spectacles of memory when we are asleep. G. de Chirico expresses as no one has done before him the pathetic melancholy of the close of a beautiful day in some ancient Italian city where, in the background of a solitary piazza, amid a décor of loggias, porticoes and monuments to the past, a train goes by emitting puffs of smoke, a department store's van is stationed and a very high chimney sends out smoke in a cloudless sky.[68]

1913: THE DEEPENING OF PERSPECTIVE

De Chirico's use of far perspective, to which his countryman, Soffici, has referred, really began in 1913. As noted, the painter had produced very few pictures during his first year and a half in Paris. In 1913 he became almost prolific. To the Salon d'Automne of this year he sent a portrait of Mme L. Gartzen (the picture has disappeared), *Etude* (which may well have been the *Nude* of 1911–12, as noted), *The Melancholy of a Beautiful Day* (page 174) and *The Rose Tower* (page 170). Related to the last-named two paintings but probably painted earlier in 1913 because of its sweeter colors is *The Delights of the Poet* (page 171), one of the first pictures of de Chirico's early career to have been seen frequently in New York exhibitions.

The building in the background of *The Delights of the Poet*, through an imaginative double-entendre, might be either a late Renaissance palace or a neo-classic railroad station. Behind it appears a ghostly locomotive, henceforth a frequent stage property in de Chirico's dream world. Was the painter's persistent use of this motif inspired by childhood memories of toy trains or by the exceptional part that travel played in his adult emotional experience? There is an authentic early drawing (page 83) in which the train seems to be a toy, and such objects may have had a special significance for him as a child, since in running toy trains he was imitating his engineer-father. On the other hand, real locomotives figure prominently in several adult dreams described by de Chirico, and during his early career he is said to have been neurotically troubled by railway travel (in his autobiography, for example, he records that he was desperately ill when journeying with his mother from Florence to Turin and from Turin to Paris).

Whatever the derivation of de Chirico's fascination with trains, their symbolic efficacy in his art is the more remarkable in that their romantic appeal is everywhere accepted to the point of banality. Indeed, the train's nostalgic hold on popular imagination has not been rivaled seriously by that of the automobile or even, thus far, that of the aeroplane (though possibly by that of the boat). Then how to explain the evocative power of trains in de Chirico's early pictures? Perhaps the answer lies in a rare kind of poetic naïveté which, like that of the Douanier Rousseau, gives commonplace objects an air of legerdemain. For de Chirico's trains are more disturbing than most Freudian symbols of malaise invented by later artists. They cut to the core of ordinary experience. Sometimes they appear in the distance, amid a silence evoking an almost physical longing for the reassurance of their sound. Then again they are animal-like, ferocious and caged, as in *The Anxious Journey* (page 181).

The foreground figure in *The Melancholy of a Beautiful Day* (page 174) once more recalls Böcklin; the statue of Ariadne, first seen in the *Melancholy* of 1912 (page 169), is given a prominent place and will soon become a central symbol in a long series of pictures (pages 174–180). But now, as to a slightly lesser degree in *The Delights of the Poet*, the use of far perspective extends throughout the major portion of the composition and is bounded this time by a landscape in the distance. The picture's vista is contained at the left by a freestanding colonnade, whose rapidly diminishing arches intensify the illusion of limitless space. Its predominant diagonal thrust at the left, also to be found in *The Delights of the Poet*, will presently be varied by an opposing architectural wing to the right, as in *The Lassitude of the Infinite* (page 175).

In *The Rose Tower* (page 170) Böcklin's shrouded figures are replaced, as psychological and spatial accents, by a mysterious box in the foreground and by rocks or bricks lying on the square like strewn relics of some ancient disaster. The technical function of the box is obvious: it helps establish the steep rise of the square or court and makes credible the composition's drastic and unlikely perspective. But what does the box contain? By whom has it been abandoned? As when painting in *The Delights of the Poet* the silent fountain whose sound we actually hear, de Chirico again displays his power to surcharge commonplace objects with a disquieting ambiguity.

At the rear of *The Rose Tower* looms a crenelated tower, sienna in color and bringing to mind a truncated version of the thirteenth-century tower at Viterbo (page 60). To the right appears one of the puzzling statues that haunt de Chirico's desolate squares. In discussing the artist's brief stay in Turin on his way to Paris, mention has already been made of his possible admiration for the equestrian monuments of Carlo Marocchetti. Referring specifically to *The Rose Tower*, de Chirico has written "In the background behind a wall, loomed an equestrian statue like the monuments to the soldiers and heroes of the Risorgimento, so ubiquitous in Italy and especially common in Turin."[69]

In Turin the principal monuments of Marocchetti are those in honor of Emanuelo Filiberto and Carlo Alberto (page 58), heroes respectively of Italy's sixteenth and nineteenth centuries. The statue of Carlo Alberto is almost certainly the one appearing in *The Rose Tower* (and again in *The Departure of the Poet*—page 190), not only because of de Chirico's reference to "soldiers and heroes of the Risorgimento," but because its Victorian realism of costume would have been more likely to appeal to the painter than Marocchetti's mid-nineteenth-century attempt to portray Filiberto in late Renaissance armor. In any case, the pedestal of de Chirico's statue in *The Rose Tower* is seen in glaring side light, while with characteristic perversity the painter renders the statue itself as a black silhouette, as if its place had been usurped by its own shadow.

The Rose Tower typifies the beginning of de Chirico's true maturity as a painter. We shall no longer find the bland, rather sweet colors used in *The Delights of the Poet* and other previous works. As de Chirico's art grew stronger, it was achieved with less and less, and a principal technical difference between his paintings of 1910–12 and those executed late in 1913 and throughout 1914, is that the pigment becomes drier and thinner, especially in the dark areas. Frequently the canvas base is very lightly covered; its texture may be both seen and felt in most cases—a fact which provides us with a valuable clue in deciding which de Chiricos are authentic works of 1913–14 and which are later copies by the artist himself or by forgers. At the same time (and this is a fundamental distinction of the painter's early art), de Chirico's color becomes more and more luminous by late 1913, as though he had learned to light his works through broad contrasts of thin tone instead of relying on surface brilliance. And if few traces of Böcklin's palette remain in *The Rose Tower* and succeeding pictures, it is interesting to note that de Chirico particularly admired the Swiss artist's reticent impasto: "With rare intelligence he exploited certain subjects, certain ingenious inventions of the ancients, *as well as the dryness of mural painting*" [author's italics].[70]

THE TOWER SERIES

Except for 1914, the year 1913 was the most prolific of de Chirico's early career and during it he developed a good part of the iconography he was to use until his return to Italy in the summer of 1915.

To the year 1913 definitely belongs the picture known as *The Great Tower* (page 173), the second in a series of three paintings of a triply colonnaded, high tower. The picture is so dated in Roman numerals, and there is every stylistic reason to suppose the date correct. But its series begins with the work called simply *The Tower* (page 172) which is related in handling to the *Nude* of late 1911 or early 1912 (page 167) and was probably executed at about the same time. Both the pictures just mentioned are grayish and somber in tonality, except for passages of bold white, and de Chirico had perhaps adopted their astringent palette as a means of breaking away (not yet decisively) from the Böcklinesque tans and blues of his 1910 works. There is a decided resemblance between the architectural passages occurring at the right in both *The Tower* and the *Nude*. The architecture itself is given little textural interest; it is defined primarily by heavy geometric contours, and its recessions are suggested by a slight variation of the pervading mouse-colored tonality.

In *The Great Tower* of 1913, the rounded campanile of *The Tower* is moved out into stronger light and to the center of the stage. The picture's foreground court seems to be a walled platform or gigantic box onto which two diminutive and shadowy figures have wandered. The tower is, of course, a free invention, identical to that in the earlier *Tower* except that its windows have been shifted slightly. Its first storey recalls the Temple of Vesta in Rome. But from this base rises a strange yet credible structure, as though a Renaissance architect had extended skywards the simple, Roman Temple of Vesta. The structure itself is more solid and real than the buildings in the scenic "wings" of *The Tower* and the *Nude*.

The tower series reaches its climax with *The Nostalgia of the Infinite* (page 53) whose inscribed date, 1911, is certainly incorrect and may have been added to its signature by the artist at the time of his 1926 exhibition at Paul Guillaume's gallery in Paris, a year after de Chirico's post-war return to the French city. It is the only work reproduced (complete with 1911 date) in the catalogue of that important exhibition, which contained a number of the painter's finest early works, and at that late date de Chirico, if he inscribed the picture then, may have had uppermost in mind the year of his first arrival in Paris, that is, 1911. *The Nostalgia of the Infinite* is in any case far too mature a work to have been finished before late 1913 or early 1914. It was first publicly exhibited at the Salon des Indépendants in the spring of 1914, together with two pictures completed during the year preceding the Salon's opening, and there is no reason to imagine that de Chirico would have held so important a painting in reserve for several years before submitting it to a major Salon. Between 1911 and the opening of the Salon des Indépendants for 1914, the artist had exhibited twice at the Salon d'Automne and once at the Indépendants.

Even more conclusive as to the true date of the *Nostalgia* is the fact that it represents so drastic an advance in conception and technique over *The Tower*, here attributed to 1911–12. It is indeed more luminous and rich than the dated *Great Tower* of 1913, and therefore was probably completed very late in 1913 or early in 1914, just before the Salon opened. The false date on the *Nostalgia* has done much to confuse the chronology of de Chirico's early career. The central structure in the *Nostalgia* is a square tower rather than a round one, as in the two previous versions of the same general subject. And the composition is more complex than in other works of the series, and includes a number of the most effective properties of de Chirico's strange world of reverie— a foreground box or abandoned van; a portico sidling into view; a shadow cast by an unseen presence; two tiny figures dwarfed by their vast setting; ghoulish, empty windows in the tower whose pennants blow vigorously amid an atmosphere otherwise totally inert. The image is especially piercing and memorable in that its thin pigment is luminous, almost incandescent, as though lighted from beneath the canvas.

If the *Nostalgia* evokes an extraordinarily dreamlike illusion of infinite space and quiet, we must not disregard the skillful plastic means through which the illusion has been achieved. Because de Chirico was intent on restoring to painting a sense of poetic mood (and this in an era when most advanced artists were bitterly repenting Romanticism's ecstasies and tears), his early art is often judged solely by lyric as opposed to classical standards, a fact about which he himself protested at the time of his first one-man show, held in Rome in 1919: "The word *metaphysics* with which I have christened my painting ever since the time when I worked in Paris during the subtle and fertile pre-war years, caused annoyance, bad humor and misunderstandings of considerable proportions among the quasi-intellectuals on the banks of the Seine. The customary sarcasm, which soon degenerated into a hackneyed phrase, was: *c'est de la littérature.*" [71]

It is true, of course, that nearly all de Chirico's early paintings are dominated by their oneirocritical content and in this sense might conceivably be thought "literary" on casual glance. But the hushed spatial serenity of the *Nostalgia* is achieved through a quite abstract handling of form, testifying to the atavistic impetus of the artist's Renaissance heritage. The image is one of the most concentrated in all de Chirico's early art. It is also an eloquent illustration of Nietzsche's theory, proposed in *The Will to Power*—"The phenomenal world is the adjusted world which we believe to be real."

THE ARIADNE SERIES

In 1913 de Chirico also painted a series of pictures in which a major iconographical role is played by a statue of Ariadne, already utilized in two prior works—*Melancholy* (page 169) and *The Melancholy of a Beautiful Day* (page 174). The statue itself (page 61) is, of course, a Roman copy of the lost Hellenistic sculpture of Ariadne asleep on the island of Naxos, where she had been abandoned by Theseus. Several of these Roman copies exist in Italy, and de Chirico would have seen either the one at Florence or the one in the Vatican.

The sculpture of Ariadne took on a profound symbolic meaning for the painter, perhaps in part because it typified the classical past to which he had so often been exposed during his childhood in Greece, in part because Nietzsche had repeatedly invoked Ariadne's name, exclaiming at one point "Who knows but me, who Ariadne is?" At any rate, Ariadne's image penetrated de Chirico's consciousness to such an extent that he himself made a small plaster variant on the recumbent Greek-Roman figure (page 61)—the only early sculpture by the artist that has thus far come to light. Like Poussin and numerous other painters of previous centuries, de Chirico may have wished to have a three-dimensional model before his eyes while working; his little sculpture's casual execution does not suggest that he intended it as an independent work of art. By the same token, his studio on the rue Campagne-Première very likely contained the plaster fragments of antique statuary which appear in other works of his first Paris period.

There are five capital de Chirico paintings of 1913 on the Ariadne theme. Of these, two—*The Soothsayer's Recompense* (page 176) and *Ariadne* (page 178)—are among the

The Nostalgia of the Infinite, 1913–14.
53¼ × 25½". The Museum of Modern
Art, New York

four known large canvases of de Chirico's early career (the other two are the *Gare Montparnasse* and *The Enigma of a Day*, pages 191 and 189).

The Soothsayer's Recompense is unique in de Chirico's early *œuvre* in that its palm trees suggest a Mediterranean setting. And while there is no certain method of establishing the chronological sequence of the five Ariadne pictures, it seems plausible to assume that this painting was among the first. Its frontal composition is related to that of certain paintings completed between 1910 and 1912, and is bare and restrained by comparison with the complex organization of *The Joys and Enigmas of a Strange Hour* (page 180), in which the Ariadne series reaches its climax. Yet we have only to compare *The Soothsayer's Recompense* with such previous pictures as *The Enigma of the Hour* (page 168) and *Melancholy* (page 169), to understand how idiosyncratic de Chirico's plastic vision has become. In the painting's background, for example, a Renaissance palace or neo-classic railroad station is seen simultaneously from the side and head-on. The shadowed inner contours of the arch at the right are willful rather than real; the jagged shadow cast by the sculpture of Ariadne is improbable by naturalistic standards. We must not, however, suppose that such distortions of truth were the result of naïveté on the artist's part, for de Chirico's technical training had been exceptionally thorough, as noted in the early pages of this book. Rather the painter had deliberately turned his back on accepted reality so as to propose a counter-logic whose impact is sharpened by jig-saw extremes of light and shade. *The Soothsayer's* memorable lyricism is achieved by dislocations quite as extreme as those in many abstract and expressionist works, and de Chirico's ingenuity of form should not be overlooked.

The horizontal plan of *The Soothsayer's Recompense* is succeeded, in *Ariadne's Afternoon* (page 179), by an exaggerated verticality of format. And the latter picture brings to view another facet of de Chirico's curious temporal sense. In the middle, flanked by a train and an old sailing vessel, rises what seems to be a modern industrial chimney, recalling the painter's contemporaneous lines, quoted by the late Paul Eluard: "A painter has painted an enormous red chimney that a poet adores like a divinity."[72] At the right of the chimney appears a stubby, medieval tower and in the foreground, of course, the antique sculpture of Ariadne. The wry assembly of such divergent temporal references—ancient, medieval, Renaissance, Victorian and modern—is often to be found in de Chirico's early art and results in a disturbingly ambiguous evocation of a sense of time. A counterplay between symbols of the past and of the present was obviously a deliberate part of the artist's dramatic program. His use of what he was to call "the new pathos"[73] combined the romantic appeal of the remote in time with that of the strictly new.

In this connection de Chirico's essay on Klinger is again extremely relevant to his own procedure as an artist. In describing the German painter's haunting admixture of temporal allusions, he declares:

Out of modern life, out of the continuous development of man's activities, out of the machinery, constructions and gadgets of everyday progress, Klinger managed to extract a romantic feeling, strange, yet deep. What is this romanticism of modern life? It is the breath of yearning that flows over the capitals of Europe, down the streets darkened by crowds, over the booming crossroads of cities, over the geometry of suburban factories, over the apartment houses that rise like cement or stone cubes, over the sea of houses and buildings, compressing within their hard flanks the sorrows and hopes of insipid daily life. It is the pretentious private residence in the breathless torpor of a springtime morning or in the moonlit calm of a summer night, with all the shutters closed behind the garden trees and the wrought-iron gates. It is the nostalgia of railroad stations, of arrivals and departures, the anxiety of seaports where ships, their hawsers loosened, sail into the black waters of the night, their lights aglitter as in cities on a holiday... Klinger was deeply conscious of the *drama of modern life* and in many of his works expressed it superbly.[74]

De Chirico himself, with far greater originality and strength than Klinger, has converted scenes and objects from the contemporary world into nostalgic complements of historical relics. If antiquity, the Middle Ages, the Renaissance and the late Victorian era are the main focal points of his visionary longing, he has reacted also and in a comparable spirit, to his own age, particularly to its industrial scenes. "From our windows which are open to Homeric dawns and to sunsets pregnant with tomorrow," he wrote in 1919, "we have the encouraging spectacle of the harbors and of the factories and of all those regularized sections in which certain suburbs make one think the sea close at hand. The howling of the factory whistles calling the men back to work brings to mind at certain fixed hours our splendid destiny of being travelers. Unknown birds from distant regions drop exhausted in our rooms after long flights across the seas."[75] Seldom since the nineteenth century's period of high romanticism has there been a more unrestrained confession of the dual attraction of the past and the present, of the near and the far. One hears a blurred echo of Baudelaire's superb rhetoric.

Whereas in *Ariadne's Afternoon* the sculpture of Ariadne is placed within a box-like, walled platform already used in *The Great Tower* (page 173) and later to recur in the artist's "metaphysical" still lifes, in *The Silent Statue* and *Ariadne* (pages 177–178) the sculpture again rests on the pavement of a piazza. For both pictures the sculptural model used must have been de Chirico's own small plaster variant on the Roman replicas of the Ariadne (page 61), since the figure's right arm is at her side and in other particulars the statue resembles the painter's little model.

The two last-named paintings between them typify the compositional ingenuity to which de Chirico progressed rapidly in 1913. In *Ariadne* the emphasis is on broad, simple and vigorous forms—a squat tower, monolithic arches, heavy geometric shadows. The bold, parallel diagonals penetrate deeply the horizontal plan; the entire center of the image is filled by a rhomboid shadow cast by the arcade at the right. But in *The Silent Statue*, de Chirico adopted a system of perspective to which he was to return at intervals, notably in the *Gare Montparnasse* (page 191). Under this system the horizontal spatial sweep is interrupted abruptly by a deep wedge into the background, asymmetrically placed, in this case consisting of a pier leading to a tower and beyond that, presumably, to the sea. But *Ariadne* and *The Silent Statue* are in other respects technically alike. Both are executed in the thin, dry manner that characterizes de Chirico's works of 1913–14; both illustrate the exceptional economy of his pictorial means. *The Silent Statue* is an especially clear illustration of the painter's linear technique. Its blocked forms are enlivened by parallel, hatched lines to suggest highlights and local shadows, by wavy lines to define the statue's drapery, and by flecked joinings and scars on the masonry surfaces. And to appreciate how thorough was de Chirico's suppression of naturalistic detail, we need only compare the tight, precise coiffure of the Roman sculpture of Ariadne with the painter's arbitrary rendering of her hair, her curls recalling the leaves of the artichokes which appear in certain of his pictures of deserted squares (pages 185–186).

The climax of the Ariadne series is reached, as briefly indicated, in *The Joys and Enigmas of a Strange Hour* (page 180). Here the statue is a fairly faithful replica of the Greek-Roman sculpture, and a new complexity and care are evident in the composition as a whole. From the freestanding, diagonal colonnade at the left, the observer's eye follows to the right the shafts of a V of strong light. The deeper shaft leads past the statue toward two diminutive figures, casting long shadows, and behind them to a remote landscape. The shorter and nearer shaft of light proceeds past the statue toward a crenelated tower with adjoining wall.

Behind the wall an old locomotive, brought to a dead halt, emits a frozen puff of smoke. The locomotive is partly concealed by the wall, as is the landscape at the extreme left of the picture. The use of walls for partial concealment, already exemplified by *The Delights of the Poet* (page 171) and several pictures in the Ariadne series, is typical of de Chirico's enigmatic vision, and once more his words on Klinger's art are pertinent to his own. In describing a Klinger landscape, he wrote: "We see some men taking a walk in the sun, their shadows fall on the ground and on a tiled wall behind them—a low and long wall. The horizon is empty. The wall seems to mark the limits of the world; there is nothing behind it. The sense of boredom and infinite apprehension, the somewhat interrogative feeling that is produced by the horizon's line—permeate the whole picture, thanks to the figures, the ground, the shadows, the light." [76]

THE ANXIOUS JOURNEY AND THE CHIMNEY

If the train in *The Joys and Enigmas of a Strange Hour* is seemingly trapped in a blind alley, its fires soon to burn out, the locomotive in *The Anxious Journey* (page 181)

Piazza San Carlo, Turin. Alinari photograph

Piazza Vittorio Emanuele, Turin. Alinari photograph

Courtyard adjoining the Brancacci Chapel,
Church of the Carmine, Florence

Marocchetti: *Monument to Carlo Alberto*, Turin, c. 1861

Monument to Giovanni Battista Bottero, Turin.
Two views

Thirteenth-century tower, Viterbo

The Castello Estense, Ferrara,
Anderson photograph

Ariadne (Roman copy of a lost Hellenistic statue). The Vatican Museum, Rome

De Chirico: *Ariadne*, c. 1913. Plaster, 6³/₄ × 22¹/₄″. Collection Jean Paulhan, Paris

De Chirico: *The Philosopher and the Poet*, 1913 (?). Pencil,
12¹/₂ x 9¹/₂". Collection Roland Penrose, London

De Chirico: *The Philosopher and the Poet*, 1915 (?). Pencil

De Chirico: *The Philosopher and the Poet*, 1915 (?). Oil on canvas,
32³/₄ × 20⁵/₈″. Collection Conte Don Alfonso Orombelli, Milan

De Chirico: *Portrait of Guillaume Apollinaire*, 1914(?). Charcoal on paper, 23¹/₂ x 21¹/₄". Collection Roland Penrose, London

Pierre Roy: Woodcut, 1914, after de Chirico's portrait of Apollinaire

Guillaume Apollinaire, c. 1916.
Photograph taken by Marcel Adéma
after the poet's trepanation

appears in a totally different guise—as an oneiric, menacing phantom, recognized suddenly, as when one is aware of a motionless snake in one's path. Or, to seek a parallel in art itself, the train in *The Anxious Journey* may be compared to the tiger in a Klinger print from the *Eve and the Future* series, which appears like an apparition at the end of a mountainous path. But de Chirico's image is far more subtle and troubling than Klinger's. The nightmarish reality of the locomotive is sharpened by its emergence at the edge of a veritable labyrinth of arches, winding in and out, leading nowhere. The painting is clearly a dream image, expressing the terror of being lost in a railroad station before an important journey, of trying desperately to locate a train, only to discover it finally at the far end of an inaccessible corridor. The psychological meaning of such a dream is, of course, a more complicated matter, not to be deciphered accurately in this case without direct psychoanalytical evidence as to the painter's state of mind—and emotion—when the image was created. But we do know that at intervals throughout his early career de Chirico's imagination became dark and troubled. Certainly *The Anxious Journey* may be described as an obsessive work; it is surpassed in capacity to disturb only by *The Child's Brain* (page 193) and *The Disquieting Muses* (page 135). Its psychological intensity is more than adequate compensation for its sketchiness and comparative technical poverty.

Could *The Anxious Journey* have been influenced by Robert Delaunay's *St. Séverin* and his other paintings of architectural subjects in which cubism's precepts are applied to a maze of Gothic forms? The theory seems plausible in view of Guillaume Apollinaire's admiration for Delaunay's art. Indeed, it is difficult to believe that Apollinaire would not have tried to communicate to his young Italian protégé some of his enthusiasm for the cubist movement as a whole. Paintings by the leading figures in the movement were hanging in the poet's apartment on the Boulevard Saint-Germain to which, as noted, de Chirico went often in 1913 and 1914. *The Anxious Journey's* dark, narrow tonal range, together with its huddled use of architectural forms, suggests that de Chirico was by now fully aware of the cubists' leadership in the vanguard of pre-war art in Paris. In slightly later works like *The Surprise* (page 192), *The Purity of a Dream* (page 215) and *The Joy of Return* (page 214), an interrelationship between de Chirico's solitary art and the group achievement of the cubists suggests itself.

In the picture known as *The Chimney* (page 182), which almost certainly once had a different and more complicated title, the square chimney of *Ariadne's Afternoon* (page 179) becomes round and the Roman statue of Ariadne is replaced by the Victorian sculpture that plays so vital a role in *The Enigma of a Day* and whose genesis will be discussed at greater length in connection with the latter picture. And in *The Chimney* there appears, presumably for the first time, a cannon—an object more conspicuously placed in *The Philosopher's Conquest* (page 188) and, as we shall see, a symbolic reference to a childhood memory of de Chirico's.

Sometime in 1913 de Chirico began to populate the foregrounds of his Italian squares with inanimate objects, while retaining his deep background perspectives. The compositional antecedents of this practice are too well known to require comment; fifteenth-century Italian painting, as an unavoidable example, includes numerous works in which foreground figures loom up before a remote landscape. But the astonishing thing about de Chirico's adaption of this traditional device is the iconographical irrelevance between the near objects and their spatial setting. The huge artichokes in *The Square* (page 185), the bananas and plaster torso in *The Uncertainty of the Poet* (page 184)—these objects look as though they had rained to earth from another, less reasonable planet. Indeed, the artist himself hinted at some such celestial source when he wrote in 1919: "The absolute realization of the space that any object should occupy in a picture and of the space that separates the various objects, establishes a new astronomy of all things which are bound to the planet by the law of gravitation."[77] And in the same article, significantly entitled "Sull' Arte Metafisica," we find perhaps the clearest explanation the artist has ever given of the "metaphysical" conception of still life which applies to many of his paintings of the early period:

Every serious work of art contains two different lonelinesses. The first might be called "plastic loneliness," that is, the beatitude of contemplation produced by the ingenious construction and combination of forms, whether they be still lifes come alive or figures become still—the double life of a still life, not as a pictorial subject, but in its supersensory aspect, so that even a supposedly living figure might be included. The second loneliness is that of lines and signals; it is a metaphysical loneliness for which no logical training exists, visually or psychically.[78]

If the appearance of commonplace vegetables and fruit amid de Chirico's melancholy squares is disquieting, it is nonetheless immediately acceptable, first because of the artist's talent for spatial organization, and, secondly, because of his genius for poetic dislocation. The latter is by far the more rare phenomenon in art, for in most cases where painters have disrupted the traditional affinities of subject matter, the new medley seems gratuitous and self-consciously fantastic (witness the pictures by imitators of the original surrealists). The violence done to logic appears arbitrary; one feels that the violence could easily have taken another and different form. Contrarily, the dislocation of reality in de Chirico's early art is convinced and unique. His still-life objects, for example, have the intensity of meaning with which children invest their playthings. In thus depicting them in strange isolation, amid far unreal perspectives, de Chirico has in effect proclaimed the validity of a counter-reality which children accept with passionate faith.

In technique the still lifes of 1913 are deceptively simple. Their thin areas of color are contained within heavy, black contours, not often to be found in the art of post-impressionism's successors. Chiaroscuro is achieved through relatively primitive linear hatchings or by means of shaded passages in which there is almost no gradation of tone. Yet a sense of physical identity is conveyed; the objects give the illusion of a precision of definition not actually theirs. The deserted, haunted squares or piazzas are inhabited by inanimate protagonists of a memorable, if inexplicable drama—solemn, piercing and more widely credible than the painter himself can have thought possible when he wrote, in 1919: "The very fact of discovering a mysterious aspect in everyday objects would be, psychically speaking, a symptom of mental abnormality related to certain phenomena of madness."[79]

The *Self Portrait* (page 183) testifies to de Chirico's rising interest in the symbolic efficacy of objects and signs; it includes plaster feet, a tubular form which might be either a fallen tower or a musical instrument somewhat like a recorder, an egg, a St. Andrew's cross and two factory chimneys. To the painter-critic, Gordon Onslow-Ford, lecturing on de Chirico's early art,* these objects symbolize the artist's progress through life. The plaster toes are read as representing de Chirico's babyhood, when his toes played a major part in his visual experience. The painter advances in age, symbolically, as we move from the foreground to the background of the canvas. Thus the factory chimneys were described by Mr. Onslow-Ford as symbols of adult virility, incomplete (i. e. cut off) in the right chimney, triumphant in the left one. The St. Andrew's cross on the wall represents de Chirico's aspiration to faith and knowledge; the egg, his renunciation and retreat from reality.

However ingenious this psychoanalytical interpretation by a sensitive artist-critic, there is no certainty, of course, that it corresponds to what de Chirico had in mind, consciously or subconsciously, when he painted the picture. Until the psychoanalytical method of iconology is more highly developed, with attendant firsthand documentation, perhaps we must be satisfied to note the drastic departure from realism which is apparent in the 1913 self portrait by comparison with earlier works in de Chirico's career, though none of the latter could be described as truly realistic.

De Chirico himself, however, has again insisted on the dual identity of certain objects in his paintings. "By deduction it is therefore possible to conclude that every object has two appearances: one, the current one, which we nearly always see and that is seen by people in general; the other a spectral or metaphysical appearance beheld only by some rare individuals in moments of clairvoyance and metaphysical abstraction, as in the case of certain bodies concealed by substances impenetrable by sunlight yet discernible, for instance, by X-ray or other powerful artificial means."[80]

The three additional pictures in the 1913 series of piazzas with still life are *The Square* (page 185), *The Uncertainty of the Poet* (page 184) and *The Transformed*

* Gordon Onslow-Ford's lecture on de Chirico's early paintings was entitled "Chirico City," and was delivered in New York City in 1943 or 1944.

Dream (page 187). The first two are correctly dated; the third, as noted briefly, is falsely inscribed 1908; its true date—1913—is clearly revealed beneath the surface dating by an infra-red photograph (page 126). *The Square* is a rather somber work, whereas *The Uncertainty of the Poet* and *The Transformed Dream* are soft and relatively lush in handling. In both the latter two paintings the yellow bananas contrast vividly with the white plaster fragments of antique sculpture which de Chirico probably kept in his studio as tangible reminders of the ancient Greece in which he had been reared. It seems likely that *The Transformed Dream* was completed late in 1913. It is close in general conception to *The Philosopher's Promenade* of 1914 (page 186), especially as to the important iconographic role assigned to a plaster head of Jupiter. This head, presiding sightless over littered fruit, affords another example of de Chirico's curious disruption of temporal logic.

1914: THE CLIMAX OF THE SERIES OF ITALIAN SQUARES

Gaining steadily in authority, de Chirico in 1914 painted such masterworks as *Mystery and Melancholy of a Street* (page 73), *The Child's Brain* (page 193) and *The Enigma of a Day* (page 189). And contrary to general belief, 1914 was the last year in which the artist used architecture as a thoroughly predominant theme. Though many pictures of Italian squares have appeared dated 1915 or even later, most if not all of them are either forgeries or copies of early works by de Chirico himself. A statement by the painter would seem to confirm this assertion. Writing in the magazine *Valori Plastici* in 1919, when the pictures of his first Paris period were presumably quite fresh in mind, de Chirico declared: "I have given a great deal of thought to the metaphysics of Italian architecture, and all my painting of the years 1910, 1911, 1912, 1913 and 1914 is concerned with this problem."[81] This is not to say, of course, that architecture ceased to play a major role in de Chirico's iconography after 1914. But with rare exceptions it thereafter tended to provide the *mise en scène* for a more and more ironic presentation of still life and, gradually, of mannequin figures. Not until the early 1920s, several years after his early, metaphysical period had come to an end, did the artist again use architecture as an almost exclusive subject matter—this time in a series of tempera paintings collectively known as "the Roman Villas" (page 139).

The brilliant picture now in the Chicago Art Institute is widely and probably correctly known as *The Philosopher's Conquest* (page 188). But the picture is reproduced as *The Joys and Enigmas of a Strange Hour* in André Breton's *Le surréalisme et la peinture* (1928)—a book which did much to re-establish the importance of de Chirico's early paintings. If we were to accept Breton's title, this would be the picture exhibited by the painter in the Salon des Indépendants of 1914, together with *The Nostalgia of the Infinite* and *The Enigma of a Day*. The writer's opinion, however, is that Breton's title should be reserved for the painting of 1913, now in the Ludington collection (page 180).

The Chicago picture constitutes a virtual anthology of de Chirico's early iconographical elements. Against the horizon appear a square-rigged ship, a train, a factory chimney and a rounded tower—all by now familiar stage properties of the painter's dream world. The clock is set at 1:28, as in the *Gare Montparnasse* (page 191). In the foreground the two artichokes of *The Square* and *The Philosopher's Promenade* confront the spectator from their boxlike pedestal. Beside them appears a cannon (already utilized in *The Chimney*) and cannon balls. The passage recalls those late Victorian military monuments which are common abroad and in this country. Yet if it were not for the fact that the First World War was still some months away, we might believe that de Chirico's cannon had some relation to current reality (in his autobiography he speaks of having been stirred, late in 1914, by the rumble of artillery moving through the Paris streets). As it is, the cannon probably derives from childhood memory. Writing about his youth in Volo at the time of the Turkish war, the painter declares: "The green, white and red flag waved from our balcony. The name of the ship was 'Vesuvio'; it was an old ship whose principal armament consisted of an enormous cannon which had to be loaded from the breach, not with a single, compact shell, but with separate explosive, missiles and percussion cap."[82]

Whether we consider the appearance of the cannon as a prophecy of war or regard it merely as a reference to childhood experience, its presence in *The Philosopher's Conquest* brings to mind a quality of de Chirico's early art which has usually been either ignored or greatly exaggerated—his eroticism. On the one hand many observers have refused to see the least sign of erotic intent in the painter's imagery; on the other, a few critics have proclaimed that his shadows and towers are phallic, his arcades vaginal, his still lifes symbolic of sex. The truth probably lies between the two theories. There is *some* eroticism in de Chirico's early works, but not as much, surely, as the extremists would have us believe. In describing what manner of eroticism this is, the words of Robert Melville seem appropriate. He called it "as subtle and innocent as Watteau's."[83] And if in relation to *The Philosopher's Conquest's* cannon and cannon balls, the word "subtle" does not seem altogether appropriate, the word "innocent" nearly always is. There is an obvious naïveté about de Chirico's perhaps unconscious preoccupation with sexual forms. He is like a child making his first confidences on the subject to someone older than he whom he must not offend and to whom he does not wish to betray the incompleteness of his knowledge. His slyness is the slyness of caution and a desire to please. When he has been unusually explicit, he changes the subject abruptly as when, in *The Philosopher's Conquest*, he diverts attention from the military monument and hurries the observer away from the scene of confession, through the circuitous corridor at the right of the canvas.

In the large painting, *The Enigma of a Day* (page 189), the foreground still life disappears. Its place is taken by a nineteenth-century sculpture of a standing, frock-coated male figure—a comparatively rare motif in authentic works of de Chirico's early career, though commonly found, with impossibly hunched shoulders, in forgeries. As noted briefly in discussing the painter's visit to Turin in 1911 (page 35), de Chirico's interest in the phantomic aspects of public statuary was probably aroused by Schopenhauer's words on the subject. After a long search in the major cities of Italy, the writer believes that the most plausible existing prototype of the sculpture in *The Enigma of a Day* (and also in *The Chimney*, page 182) is the monument to the philosopher, Giovanni Battista Bottero, which stands in Turin's Largo Quattro Marzo (page 59). The image of Bottero may have been combined in memory with, among others, those of Quintino Sella at Turin and of Cosimo Ridolfi at Florence. Yet it is reasonable to suppose, in view of de Chirico's passion for metaphysics, that he would have remembered most poignantly a monument to a philosopher—Bottero. At any rate, when the statue reappears in *The Serenity of the Scholar* (page 195), it is altered in pose. In other paintings, the sculpture is hidden by architecture and only its cast shadow warns of its presence, as in *The Mystery and Melancholy of a Street* (page 73).

That the frock-coated statue has been included often in forgeries of de Chirico's early works, must be due to the fact that *The Enigma of a Day* played so crucial a part in the surrealist movement which brought the artist a truly international fame. The picture was an important visual backdrop to the intense surrealist activity of the years 1924 to 1935. During that decade it hung in the apartment of surrealism's overlord, André Breton. Breton and his colleagues were frequently photographed in front of the large canvas, and in *Le surréalisme au service de la révolution* they published replies to a questionnaire in which members of the surrealist group were asked to decipher and locate various objects, both real and illusory, within the painting.[84] The replies no less than the questions were extremely subjective, as might be expected. They nevertheless furnish impressive proof of the picture's hold on surrealist thought and reverie. To Breton and his associates, *The Enigma of a Day* typified an inhabitable dream. Its silence and eerie light established the mood of a great deal of subsequent surrealist art; its drastic elongations of perspective, exemplified by the abrupt scaling-down of the background figures in relation to the foreground sculpture, became a recurrent poetic device in the paintings of Tanguy, Dali, Magritte, Delvaux and numerous other surrealists of a slightly later generation. Indeed, in every direction except that of automatism (the free-wheeling inventions of Miro, Masson & Co.), this and other paintings of de Chirico's early career opened the way to surrealist art in general (see pages 149–152). These paintings served as well to encourage a revival of atmospheric effect and human sentiment among the Parisian neo-romantic painters of the mid-1920s—Bérard, Tchelitchew, Berman, Léonid.

In *The Departure of the Poet* (page 190) de Chirico's reincarnation of one of Carlo Marocchetti's nineteenth-century equestrian monuments at Turin (page 58) emerges from the shadows of the surrounding architecture, which had partially concealed it in *The Rose Tower*, and is seen at a far point on the square. Behind the statue appears that low, gray, hilly, back-lit landscape which is a common terminus of vision in the painter's early compositions. An unseen factory chimney casts its long shadow at the right; the familiar train lurks in the extreme foreground instead of in its usual distant place. At the left recurs the long diagonal colonnade of *The Enigma of a Day*, though here supplied with balcony and extra windows.

The areas of light and shade on the piazza of *The Departure of the Poet* are rigidly angular, whereas in *The Anguish of Departure* (page 194), as in *The Enigma of a Day*, the court is bounded by a curved wall. An underlying geometric scheme is apparent in nearly all of de Chirico's paintings of Italian squares. But the variations within the scheme are more extensive and complicated than generally supposed.

In *The Enigma of a Day*, for example, the deep perspective radiates in pie-shaped wedges of light and shade from a center at the extreme lower left of the composition and is contained by a curve, as in geometric sectors of a circle. In the *Gare Montparnasse* (page 191)—also sometimes called *The Melancholy of Departure*—sharp, oblique angles, on the contrary, entirely determine the allocation of light and shade. And in his handling of perspective in this picture, de Chirico deliberately takes extreme liberties. The broad, receding path of light at the right retains its parallel borders to its end instead of narrowing to a point, as science and pictorial tradition demand. The psychological justification of the distortion is apparent. Failing to find a terminating point in space, the observer's eye is forced to follow the bright ramp downward again, toward the vertical piers and odd geometric forms of the lower level. How deep is the overhang of the upper platform which rests at the right on weirdly slanting pillars? At one point, directly beneath the clock, an answer is supplied by a single black line. Elsewhere the measure of depth is thoroughly ambiguous; geometry has been wilfully altered for purposes of poetic suggestion.

The Gare Montparnasse is unique in de Chirico's early *œuvre* in that it overtly depicts a modern, commercial structure, drastically rebuilt in recent years. Yet in its atmosphere of timelessness the image evokes a sense of a remote, hushed past quite as forcefully as those paintings in which the artist refers, however obliquely, to medieval, Renaissance or neo-classic buildings. And what a strange vision this is! In the foreground a bunch of green bananas inhabits an enclosed wasteland of concrete and iron, without plausible exit. This is a station at which presumably no trains will arrive, from which none will depart. The train in the background is distant and stalled, approached only by the two ghosts of travelers who have climbed the steep ramp, one imagines, only to abandon hope. The silence and inertia are absolute. The picture, as the writer has pointed out elsewhere,[85] is the absolute antithesis of paintings by the Italian Futurists in which the commotion and excitement of travel are feverishly suggested.

According to legend, de Chirico at this phase of his career was desperately homesick for Italy and thought often of returning there, only to lose hope because of the costs and complexities of the journey. Certainly the *Gare Montparnasse* is uncannily effective as a dream image of the longings and frustrations of a trip planned by rail (the Montparnasse station was the one nearest to de Chirico's studio). Like *The Anxious Journey* (page 181), it conveys the torment of nightmares in which a train must be caught for reasons of exceptional importance. But the *Gare Montparnasse* also suggests the calm which comes to the traveler when hope of reaching the platform on time has been abandoned, when there is nothing to do but wait for the hours to become meaningful again. The picture's ambivalence of mood is characteristic of de Chirico's early art as a whole. Indeed, metamorphoses of mood are among this art's rarest virtues. Moreover, even in a physical sense de Chirico's paintings, sparsely achieved as to technique, have an extraordinary capacity to change in color and light, when looked at under varying conditions. To borrow a phrase from the terminology of photographic chemistry, they tend to "come up" in detail and then to recede in brilliance. They do not so much propose metamorphosis by lyric allusion as they seem themselves to undergo it in actuality. They are for this reason, among others, far more disturbing than paintings by certain surrealist artists in which one set of appearances has been superimposed on another. They are *trompe l'œil*, that is to say, in spirit rather than handling.

THE MYSTERY AND MELANCHOLY OF A STREET; THE CHILD'S BRAIN

Two de Chirico paintings of 1914 must be considered apart from the others, due to their special and unique iconography. These are *The Mystery and Melancholy of a Street* (opposite) and *The Child's Brain* (page 193).

The former of these pictures is distinguished from all other authentic paintings of Italian squares by the presence of the girl rolling a hoop. The painter himself must have attached no particular importance to this figure, since it does not occur again except in forgeries or later copies of his early works. To many people, however, the figure of the girl is an unforgettable invention; it is by now deeply imbedded in public consciousness, like Dali's famous limp watches. And there is in fact an extreme fascination in following the girl's progress within the image. She must run for the open light, past a yellow carnival wagon (an object several times included in de Chirico's paintings of 1914), past a menacing arcade, past the forbidding shadow of a Victorian sculpture lying directly in her path. One has the impression that even if she reaches the light, she

OPPOSITE: *The Mystery and Melancholy of a Street*, 1914. 34¼ x 28⅛". Collection Stanley R. Resor, New Canaan, Connecticut

is doomed, for she is herself a shadow, perhaps retracing the steps which led to her dissolution, her image invested with the horror of ghostly re-enactment. No other painting by de Chirico more piercingly conveys the sense of omen which the painter himself once described as follows: "One of the strangest and deepest sensations that prehistory has left with us is the sensation of foretelling. It will always exist. It is like an eternal proof of the senselessness of the universe. The first man must have seen auguries everywhere, he must have trembled at each step he took."[86]

In the first version of this book (1941), it was suggested that the girl with the hoop in *The Mystery and Melancholy of a Street* might have been inspired by a similar child with streaming hair in Seurat's *La Grande Jatte* (the latter child's hoop is not visible but her gestures indicate its presence). If this conjecture is true, then de Chirico must have been one of the first to discover what becomes more and more apparent: that Seurat's paintings, quite apart from their formal virtues, are among the most enigmatic in nineteenth-century art. De Chirico's imaginative, fantastic mind would have prepared him for such a discovery even at a time when prevailing interpretations of Seurat's importance were opposite in character. Before the First World War Seurat's pictures were admired by the cubists and other abstract artists for their static design or, in the case of the Italian Futurists, for their capacity to suggest successive aspects of objects and figures in motion.[87] But de Chirico may well have appreciated Seurat for a totally different reason. If he adapted the figure of the girl with hoop from *La Grande Jatte,* he very probably recognized the hallucinatory power of those Seurat paintings in which the protagonists appear to have been brought to a dead halt with troubling abruptness, like figures in a motion picture film that has suddenly ceased to turn on its sprockets. De Chirico may have marveled at the curious impression Seurat's figures sometimes give of having been buried for centuries, of having been inexplicably revealed by a cleft in ancient terrain. His attitude toward the great neo-impressionist master, if correctly summarized here, is an additional indication of how solitary his position was in the Paris of 1911–14.

The Child's Brain (page 193) is one of the most implacable images in de Chirico's early art. It is usually accepted as a portrait of the artist's father, motivated by child-hood fears of parental authority. The figure is terrifying in its flabby pallor and in the hideous masculinity of its jet-black moustache, eyelashes and hair. Its eyes are closed, as Robert Melville has said, "for the simple reason that the child (de Chirico) would not dare to look if they were open."[88] Its square torso, with long dough-like arms prophetic of the painter's later mannequin figures, presses forward against a green table. On the table appears a yellow-brown book, closed on a scarlet marker. And whatever the shortcomings of a psychoanalytical reading of iconography without supplementary evidence from firsthand sources, perhaps we must in this case accept the widely held theory that the book and marker symbolize the father's desire and the mother's acquiescence. The theory is confirmed by the placing of the marker in relation to the torso; the entire picture is fraught with a Freudian malaise.

The background of *The Child's Brain* is painted a resonant black, relieved at the right by a high, open window through which are seen a bright red chimney (phallic echo of the book marker), a gray building and blue sky. At the left there is a heavy curtain which is closely related in tone to the naked flesh of the figure. Quite apart from its compositional function, the curtain proves de Chirico's ability to curb the emotional impact of his art at its limits of pictorial coherence, before it degenerates into hysteria. One can endure no more of this frightful commentary on parenthood and the painter knows it. If the figure's right arm were shown, or more of its bulging torso, the image would lose tension and gain only the more limited fury of caricature. As it is, the effigy of the father looms forward relentlessly, its face defined by deep incisions of line which such artists as Antonello da Messina and Botticelli had presumably taught their distant heir to utilize. There is a new richness of impasto in the handling of the figure's arm and torso—the beginning perhaps of the more sensuous technique to which de Chirico turned the following year (1915) and, with growing emphasis, in 1916 and 1917. But technical analysis is of minor value in assessing *The Child's Brain's* malignant power to strike and hold. This assuredly is one of the most alarming (in the literal sense of the word) paintings in the long history of art.

THE STILL LIFES WITH GLOVE AND ARROW

During 1914 de Chirico continued to paint architectural subjects, as in *The Surprise* (page 192), a picture so densely organized that its composition may more easily be read in a preliminary sketch (page 85). But he also resumed his interest in still life. And whereas in the 1913 paintings of deserted squares with inanimate objects, still life had remained for the most part an accessory to architecture, now it began to do more than decorate or disturb his strange settings, growing larger in scale and importance. Moreover, the very character of his still-life vocabulary tended to become more exotic. During the previous year he had mostly confined himself to plaster fragments of statuary and such homely edibles as fruit and vegetables. In 1914 he added cryptic objects, seen or imagined on his solitary walks through the streets of Paris.

The change is apparent in the most widely reproduced of his 1914 still lifes—*The Song of Love* (page 77), whose insolent and gratuitous juxtaposition of a surgeon's rubber glove with a plaster head of the Apollo. Belvedere summarized for many slightly later painters of surrealist tendency that need for a drastic reshuffling of reality to which Lautréamont had referred in the famous proto-surrealist sentence, "Beautiful as the chance meeting on a dissecting table of a sewing machine and an umbrella."

The picture's efficacy in this regard has been rivaled only by that of *The Sacred Fish* (page 155), with the difference to be noted that the latter painting's influence seems to have been greatest among Central European and Italian artists, while *The Song of Love*'s effect was widely felt in the North. This is perhaps natural in that *The Song of Love* was painted—and remained until quite recently—in Paris, whereas *The Sacred Fish* was executed in Italy after the First World War and was included in an exhibition, organized by the publishing firm of *Valori Plastici*, which was circulated in Southern and Central Europe. According to the painter Max Ernst, it was *The Sacred Fish* which helped propel him and numerous other German and Swiss Dadaists in the direction of surrealism. On the other hand, *The Song of Love* was avidly admired and emulated in Belgium and France. As an example, the critic and dealer, E. L. T. Mesens, has described what the picture meant to himself and to his friend and countryman, the painter René Magritte: "Soon after (around 1919) a reproduction of *The Song of Love* by de Chirico fell into our hands. We were fascinated. Several days later Magritte discovered in a shop a booklet published by *Valori Plastici* and devoted to the same painter. A unique emotion engulfed us. The encounter with the work of de Chirico was so overwhelming that it determined the point of departure for Magritte's research."[89]

The derivation of the glove motif in *The Song of Love* is a rather complex matter. As mentioned, the glove is a rubber one such as surgeons wear. De Chirico may well have seen its prototype in a pharmacy window, together with the anatomical charts which appear in several of his pictures. Such objects may have had a particular interest for the painter in that he himself still suffered from chronic intestinal disorders and is said by friends to have been something of a hypochondriac.

We should remember, however, that de Chirico had had in mind the fetishistic attributes of gloves ever since his student days in Munich. At that time, as noted, he had greatly admired Max Klinger's series of etchings, *Paraphrase on the Finding of a Glove* (pages 22–23). In these etchings a glove plays an active symbolic part; its appearances and disappearances provide the tempestuous scenario of a love story. The glove in de Chirico's painting, *The Song of Love*, is also the inanimate protagonist of a fantastic drama, its fellow-actors being a plaster head, a green ball and silent witnesses—architecture and a train.

De Chirico's still-life drama has no traceable plot, of course; its impact derives from the mystery of assortment of the various elements. But it conveys a considerable sense of shock, and one is again reminded of the words of Guillaume Apollinaire: "To describe the fatal character of contemporary things, the painter [de Chirico] uses that most modern recourse—surprise."[90] And what makes de Chirico's disruption of conventional reality so memorable in *The Song of Love*, is that it is regulated by a severe,

OPPOSITE: *The Song of Love*, 1914. 28³/₄ x 23¹/₂". Collection Nelson A. Rockefeller, New York City

underlying plastic discipline. The counter-logic of the young Italian artist's iconography has been imitated by numerous painters but seldom with a conviction comparable to his.

In two other 1914 paintings of still life with architecture a different kind of glove makes its appearance, and to its prototype in existing reality the painter has made specific reference. This is the metal glove whose shadow is cast on the white wall at the left in both *The Destiny of a Poet* (page 196) and *Still Life: Turin, Spring* (page 197). After the First World War, living in Italy and recalling with arrogant bitterness the loneliness of his pre-war career in Paris, de Chirico wrote:

All around me the international gang of *modern* painters slogged away stupidly in the midst of their sterile formulas and arid systems. I alone, in my squalid studio in the rue Campagne-Première, began to discern the first ghosts of a more complete, more profound and more complicated art, an art which was—to use a word which I am afraid will give a French critic an attack of diarrhea—more *metaphysical*.

New lands appeared on the horizon.

The huge zinc colored glove, with its terrible golden finger-nails, swinging over the shop door in the sad wind blowing on city afternoons, revealed to me, with its index finger pointing down at the flagstones of the pavement, the hidden signs of a new melancholy.[91]

There can be little question that the metal glove de Chirico thus describes is the one appearing in silhouette in *The Destiny of a Poet* and in *Still Life: Turin, Spring*. The glove also appears, tilted sideways, in a drawing (page 83) from which a painting was apparently never made, and also perhaps, though here in substance rather than shadow, in *The Enigma of Fatality* (page 198). In the two paintings just discussed, we find the closed book from *The Child's Brain* (page 193) and the egg already seen in the symbolic self portrait of 1913 (page 183). The *Still Life: Turin, Spring* also includes an artichoke (an object made familiar in de Chirico's art by certain paintings of 1913-14) and, at the left, part of a silhouetted equestrian monument based on Marocchetti's sculptures at Turin.

In both *The Destiny of a Poet* and *Still Life: Turin, Spring*, the still-life objects are placed on triangular platforms in the foreground. The platforms do not seem to rest on an over-all ground level, as in *The Transformed Dream* (page 187), but instead form a second and higher level, different from that on which rise the buildings in the backgrounds. An illusion of puppet-theatre artificiality results—deliberately suggested, of course. The illusion is strengthened by the toy-like character of the buildings which look as though they had been moved into place by a child standing beside a table or box above the floor on which they rest. Later on de Chirico was to complicate still further his new, seesaw use of perspective, and background street levels would be viewed from a high, foreground sill. But there is already a considerable technical difference, as to perspective, between *The Destiny of a Poet* and the *Still Life: Turin, Spring* and, for example, *The Departure of the Poet* (page 190) and *The Enigma of a Day* (page 189), with their deep, one-level stretches of paving or ground.

The difference becomes even more apparent if we compare any typical picture in the 1913–14 Italian square series with a third still-life-with-architecture, *The Fête Day* (page 199). In the latter picture the egg reappears but is juxtaposed with the scroll or recorder of the symbolic self portrait (page 183), while the downward-pointing shadow of the metal hand in *The Destiny of a Poet* and *Still Life: Turin, Spring* has been replaced by a black arrow. The architecture in the background of *The Fête Day* is nearly identical to that in *Still Life: Turin, Spring*. But in the foreground the architectural distortions are far more extreme. Though the doorway at the right is obliquely slanted, the interior window of the room to which it leads is conventionally vertical. What manner of corridor is this, from which the walls tip so abruptly away? The image is more arbitrary in its shifts of perspective than any of de Chirico's previous works, foretelling subsequent developments in his "metaphysical" art.

A possible explanation for the painter's rising tendency to abstract and flatten his architectural forms may well be that he had become impressed by the current cubist pictures of Picasso and Braque, just as previously he may have come to admire the art of Delaunay, as suggested in discussing *The Anxious Journey*. Yet the influence of cubism on de Chirico's early paintings should not be exaggerated and the statement of a Swiss painter-critic, that in the *Gare Montparnasse* "the irrational dream-state hides itself under the cubist super-structure,"[92] seems extreme. Yet if de Chirico's conception of geometric forms owes more to the philosophy of Otto Weininger than to the structural principles of Cézanne, there is no denying the stylistic affinity of works like *The Fête Day* with cubist pictures in which flat, arbitrary planes are brought forward on the canvas. De Chirico's occasional new tendency to qualify in the cubist direction the deep linear perspective on which he had once relied entirely, reaches its climax in certain still lifes of 1917 like *The Scholar's Playthings* (page 238).

Further proof of de Chirico's philosophical attitude toward geometry is supplied by *The Enigma of Fatality* (page 198), in which the metal hand of *The Destiny of a Poet* is converted into a gauntlet (now a substance rather than a shadow) and placed on a checkered flooring. The painting's format is extremely odd. Triangular pictures had, of course, been produced in previous centuries, but usually as part of a planned decorative scheme. As far as is known, however, *The Enigma of Fatality* was created as an independent easel work; its format was probably selected as part of de Chirico's announced ambition to rid art "of all that has been its familiar content until now."[93]

In this ambition the triangle plays a major part. The form recurs persistently within de Chirico's early compositions and regarding it he has written as follows: "Often in the past geometrical figures have been interpreted as portentous symbols of a higher reality. In antiquity, for instance, and now in theosophic doctrine, the triangle is considered a mystic and magic symbol, and beyond question it arouses in the beholder, even when he is ignorant of its significance, a feeling of apprehension, perhaps even of fear. (This is why draftsmen's triangles haunted me in the past and still do; I used to see them rise like mysterious stars beyond each of my pictorial images.)" [94]

We know from other early pronouncements by the artist that he wished art to regain its power as a stimulus to deep and unexpected emotion. He obviously wanted his own paintings to satisfy more urgent needs than those of the esthetic tastes of connoisseurs, and in this ambition he took part in a general twentieth-century reaction against the "art appreciation" of the previous, Victorian era. De Chirico probably shared that contempt for the *objet d'art* for its own sake which prompted his French contemporary, Marcel Duchamp, to send ready-made objects to exhibitions of painting and sculpture, as a protest against the bourgeoisie's pious veneration for hand-painted oils. By flouting stock proportions in his canvases, de Chirico may have hoped to restore to art its miraculous impact, its capacity to fix and hold our attention urgently. At any rate, *The Enigma of Fatality* is an extreme example of his tendency to achieve his curious and troubling spatial dramatics within a challenging format. The title of the picture, as noted in passing (page 46), occurs in the painter's own unpublished manuscript of c. 1913 (Appendix B), and is convincing proof that the names of most of his authentic early pictures were self-invented, though some were imitated and vulgarized by dealers and other owners through whose hands these pictures have passed.

THE APOLLINAIRE PORTRAIT AND RELATED WORKS

Mention has already been made of the *Portrait of Guillaume Apollinaire* (page 201). We do not know at precisely what point in 1914 the portrait was completed, though Pierre Roy's woodcut from it was ready by September (see page 45). In any case, the picture includes a free-standing, slanting, box-like structure quite different from the flat board or canvas to which a rubber glove, a plaster head of Apollo and a pin are affixed in *The Song of Love* (page 77). To the wide front edge of the slanting structure in the Apollinaire portrait are attached tin molds such as children use to make figures in the sand—a fish and a purely decorative form. The fish mold recurs in two other paintings of 1914—*The Dream of the Poet* (page 200) and *The Span of Black Ladders* (page 203).

The first of these two pictures is sometimes mistakenly described as a second portrait of Apollinaire, since in it reappears in the foreground a sculptured head wearing dark glasses. Eyeglasses at this point had apparently taken on a symbolic significance for the painter; a pair of such glasses occupies a central place in *The Serenity of the Scholar* (page 195), and the careful observer will note that even the statue in *The Enigma of a Day* (page 189) wears glasses.

At this point, too, de Chirico had invented another of those wry juxtapositions in which he delighted: sculpture combined with anatomical models as in *I'll be there...*

De Chirico: *The Autumn Arrival*, 1913. Pencil. Formerly collection Paul Eluard, Paris

De Chirico: *The Slumber*, 1913. Pencil, 6³/₄ x 9". Collection Mme Simone-Collinet, Paris

De Chirico: *Drawing*, c. 1913. Pencil, 7¹/₂ x 10⁵/₈". Collection Jean Paulhan, Paris

De Chirico: *Drawing*, c.1913. Pencil.
Collection Mme Edith Boissonnas, Paris

De Chirico: *The Apparition of the Horse*, 1913.
Ink? Collection Wolfgang Paalen, Paris

De Chirico: *The Enigma of the Horse*,
c.1913. Pencil, 11³/₄ x 7¹/₈".
Collection Jean Paulhan, Paris

De Chirico: *Joy*, 1913. Pencil, 6¹/₂ × 8¹/₂".
Collection Roland Penrose, London

De Chirico: *Drawing*, 1914. Pencil,
7 × 5¹/₂". Collection Jean Paulhan, Paris

De Chirico: *Drawing*, c.1913. Pencil, 14³/₄ × 12¹/₈". Collection Jean
Paulhan, Paris

De Chirico: *The Surprise*, 1914. Pencil. Formerly collection André Breton, Paris

De Chirico: *Mannequin (Morte del Milione)*, 1918. Pencil.

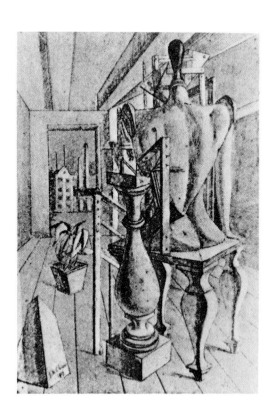

De Chirico: *The Faithful Servitor*, 1917. Pencil.

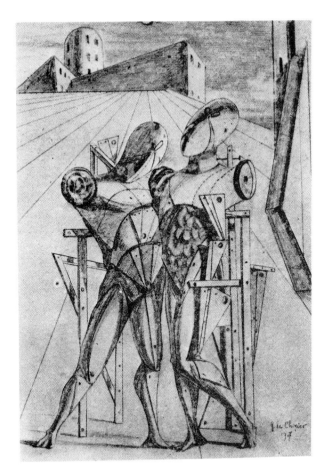

De Chirico: *The Duet*, 1917. Pencil. Formerly collection
Mario Broglio, Rome

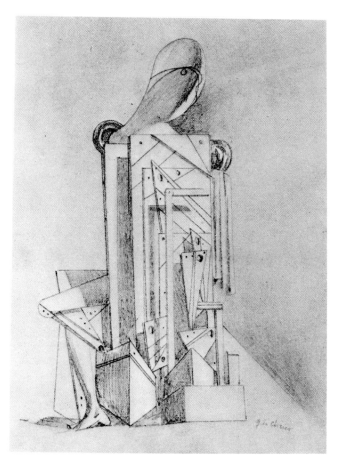

De Chirico: *The Condottiere*, 1917. Pencil. Private collection,
New Canaan, Conn.

De Chirico: *Solitude*, 1917. Pencil. Collection Paul W. Cooley, Hartford, Connecticut

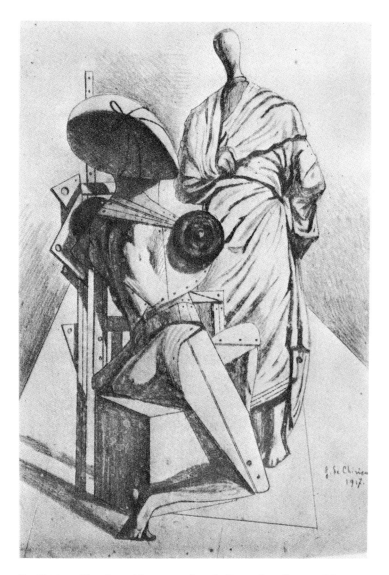

De Chirico: *The Apparition*, 1917. Pencil. Formerly collection Mario
Broglio, Rome

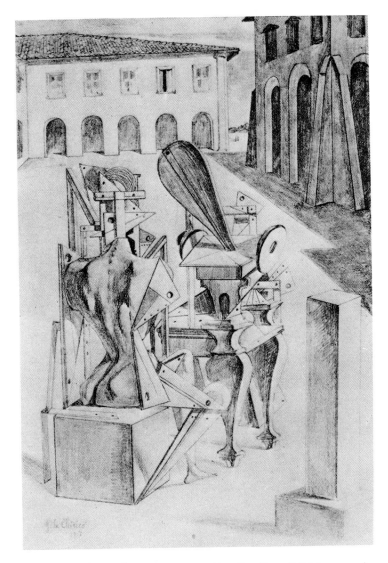

De Chirico: *The Mathematicians*, 1917. Pencil, 12⅝ x 8⅝". Museum of Modern Art, New York. Gift of Mrs. Stanley Resor

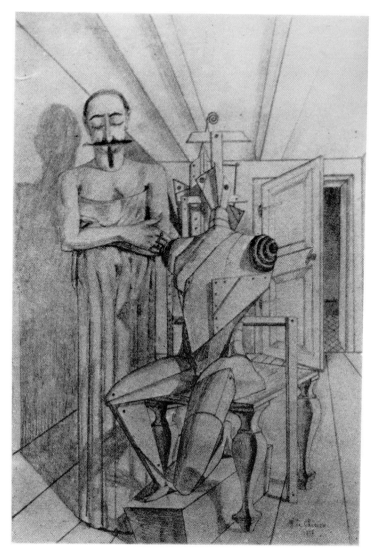

De Chirico: *The Return*, 1917. Pencil. Private collection, Italy

De Chirico: *Metaphysical Interior*, 1917. Pencil. Formerly collection
Mario Broglio, Rome

De Chirico: *Autumnal Geometry*, 1917. Pencil. Formerly collection Mario
Broglio, Rome

De Chirico: *Metaphysical Consolation*, 1918. Pencil. Formerly collection
Mario Broglio, Rome

De Chirico: *The Return of the Prodigal*, 1917. Pencil, 12³/₈ x 8". Collection Herbert Rothschild, Kitchawan, N. Y.

The Glass Dog (page 202) and *The Span of Black Ladders* (page 203)—two paintings whose titles are especially puzzling and provocative. To offset the cold surfaces of sculpture with inanimate models of living organs, sinews and veins, was to wrench logic in a thoroughly Chiricoesque manner.

In both the paintings just mentioned and also in *The Dream of the Poet* and *The Endless Voyage* (page 205), occur those enigmatic graphs and signs, black on white or white on black, which the artist will henceforth use frequently. Among them is a curious encircled triangle, with dangling hook, putting one in mind of a Calder mobile or of an illustration in a book on mechanical drawing, geometry or engineering. The form is seen most clearly above the left shoulder of the outlined figure in *I'll be there ... The Glass Dog* and at the left of the anatomical hand in *The Span of Black Ladders*. What this and other graphs mean is a mystery, though some reference to mathematical instruments seems likely. The theory gains credibility in that de Chirico was fond of such instruments. To give an example, he used a compass in drawing the round epaulets of the mannequin figures in *The Duo* (page 213), as macrophotographs of the picture make clear. And in *The Seer* (page 104), the architectural perspective in the drawing on the blackboard may also have been done with mechanical aids.

THE EVOLUTION OF THE MANNEQUIN THEME

At some point in 1914 de Chirico began to develop one of the major themes of his early art—the mannequin figure. The Italian critic, Raffaele Carrieri, has suggested[95] that the painter's interest in this curious subject matter was aroused by a play, *Les chants de la mi-mort*, written by de Chirico's brother Andrea (Alberto Savinio) and published in Apollinaire's magazine, *Les soirées de Paris*, for July–August, 1914. The drama's protagonist is a "man without voice, without eyes or face."[96] Of this mannequin-like figure Andrea is said to have made a sketch, as Jarry had done for his *Ubu Roi*, a play by which Savinio was unquestionably influenced. The sketch might have interested de Chirico as a plastic and metaphysical conception, and we must remember that the relationship between the de Chirico brothers was extremely close during their early years in Paris.

Carrieri's theory is ingenious and was confirmed by the late Alberto Savinio himself in conversations with the writer at Milan in 1948. Yet it seems probable that de Chirico's interest in mannequins was not merely the result of sudden literary inspiration. It may in fact stem from some such simple cause as that suggested by Pierre Courthion: "He runs to a shop to buy a mannequin and his inventive spirit takes form."[97] Its beginnings, indeed, may be traced back to the group of pictures related to the portrait of Apollinaire, a group which may well have been completed or at least begun before Savinio's play was published. (We do not, as noted, know the exact date in 1914 of the Apollinaire portrait. And since the poet almost certainly did not pose for so anti-realistic a portrait, there will probably be little to learn about the exact date of the picture when Apollinaire's notebooks are published in full.)

In one painting belonging to the Apollinaire portrait group, namely *I'll be there . . . The Glass Dog* (page 202), there appears at the right, as if drawn on a blackboard, the by now familiar outline of a standing Victorian statue. The statue is no longer presented as if it were of stone but as if it were a stuffed cloth figure with sewn seams. We are perhaps at the beginning here of that metamorphosis from sculpture into mannequin, soon to take place in de Chirico's iconography. In *The Dream of the Poet* (page 200), for example, the outlined figure of *I'll be there . . . The Glass Dog* becomes three-dimensional in form; its head seems to be made of stitched leather or cloth.

In 1914 de Chirico also produced two paintings of a draped, armless female figure, with the black outline of a single-eyed mask bound around her featureless face. These pictures are *The Endless Voyage* (page 205) and *The Torment of the Poet* (page 204). In the former painting the figure is depicted as a drawn image on a canvas within the canvas; in the latter the figure stands between background architecture and a foreground medley of still-life elements—a paper hat, a ball and an epaulet-like form which echoes the shoulder pieces of the figure itself.

The Endless Voyage includes the up-staring classical head of *The Span of Black Ladders* (page 203) and the latter picture's mathematical graphs, shown in this instance as white chalk drawings on a blackboard. The blackboard is supported by a wooden armature, a form which will be used with increasing complexity in de Chirico's metaphysical still lifes of 1916 and 1917, executed at Ferrara. Moreover, as noted, the mannequin is rendered as a painting-within-the-painting and, similarly, the architecture and clouds at the left are not part of an over-all architectural scene but comprise the decorated surface of a separate box or panel. This device (the picture-within-the-picture) will become a frequent element in the art de Chirico produced after his return to Italy in the summer of 1915.

THREE STILL LIFES OF 1914-15

De Chirico did not fully develop the mannequin theme until 1915. Meanwhile he had begun a series of three still lifes whose objects are especially cryptic. The series includes *The Sailors' Barracks* (page 207), *The General's Illness* (page 206) and *The Evil Genius of a King* (opposite). All three of these pictures are related in compositional formula to the *Still Life: Turin, Spring* (page 197) and *The Fête Day* (page 199) in that their foreground areas rise steeply, forming a sort of ramp or platform high above the background street level with architecture. These paintings, instead of enticing the observer

OPPOSITE: *The Evil Genius of a King*, 1914–15. 24 x 19³/₄″. The Museum of Modern Art, New York

to enter an illusory, over-all picture space, as in the earlier series of Italian squares, force him to climb to a dizzy vantage point above the ground.

All three paintings in the series under discussion include a standing, vertical board, like that in *The Song of Love* (page 77) but swung sideways, which divides their compositions asymmetrically; their still-life vocabulary is, as noted, unusually fantastic. If certain objects in them may be identified with some degree of certainty, others seem thoroughly "unreal." The ball, tube and shuttlecock or paper hat in *The General's Illness*; the epaulet, egg, ball, baton, pipe and checkerboard of *The Sailors' Barracks*; the party favors, ball and flower of *The Evil Genius of a King*— these are objects such as de Chirico might have seen on his solitary walks through Paris. But other still-life forms seem to have little basis in tangible reality. In both cases the objects are depicted with extreme precision and for a definite reason. Just as the cubists at this time were affixing sand, bits of string and other commonplace materials to their canvases in order to affirm an essential contact with reality, so de Chirico was eager to propose his fantasies in the most convincing possible manner. But above all he wished the poetry of his art to consist in unexpected juxtapositions taking place in an unlikely locale. He must have conceived of the artist's function as that of documenting metaphysical shifts in the continuity of everyday, settled reality. Apollinaire's respect for the element of "surprise" in painting again comes to mind.

At this point it may be well to digress for a moment to consider wherein de Chirico's still lifes, discussed above, differ from the "rococo" cubism being created simultaneously by his great colleague, Picasso. In 1914 both de Chirico and Picasso were intent on substituting new combinations for traditional juxtapositions of objects in still life; the latter's sculpture of this year, *The Glass of Absinthe*, is a conspicuous case in point. Their methods of so doing, however, were quite opposite. Picasso's choice of objects was based on an extraordinary visual sensitivity, whereby all manner of trite materials suggested to him the place they might find in a new, spontaneous, plastic order. He invented as he went along, guided by a sure associational instinct, as when, in *The Glass of Absinthe*, the top of the sculpture consists of a metal spatula or spoon. De Chirico, on the other hand, appears to have relied on a more or less total inspiration which he ecstatically transferred to canvas. He makes the matter clear in the following statement: "The revelation we have of a work of art, the conception of a picture *must* represent something which has no sense in itself, has no subject, which from the point of view of human logic *means nothing at all*. I say that such a revelation (or if you like, conception), must be felt so strongly, must give us such joy or such pain that we are obliged to paint, impelled by a force greater than the force which impels a starving man to bite like a wild beast into the piece of bread he happens to find."[98]

Thus while Picasso's prime creative asset was perhaps his visual alertness, that of de Chirico was his susceptibility to a kind of self-hypnosis. Picasso's control can almost never be questioned. He was and is a great artist who has made creative accidents happen almost at will, a professional born to his art and incredibly deft. De Chirico, contrarily, seems helplessly involved in the strange happenings of his genius, an amateur delighted by bewildering success. One feels that he has watched the objects accumulate in *The Evil Genius of a King* as a child watches the contents of a Christmas stocking pour out on the floor, not knowing what will come next and exclaiming at the miracle of what has already appeared.

The Evil Genius of a King is far stronger and brighter in color than the still lifes and architectural scenes of 1913 and early 1914; it is in fact more brilliant in tone than many of the paintings de Chirico was to complete at Ferrara in 1916 and 1917. Quite likely the picture was completed very late in 1914 or early in 1915. Indeed, its title and those of *The General's Illness* and *The Sailors' Barracks* suggest that all three works were painted after the outbreak of war in August, 1914. De Chirico speaks in his autobiography of his shock and horror at the advent of war, and the ironic titles of the three still lifes may allude, however indirectly, to the events at hand.

1915: CONTINUATION OF THE MANNEQUIN SERIES

In describing his activity during the early months of 1915 de Chirico has declared: "During the winter of 1914–15 I kept working at my metaphysical pictures but of course, because of abnormal conditions, this movement in painting had come to a standstill." [99] Yet the fact is that if de Chirico produced few pictures in the anxious climate of 1915's winter and spring, among them are some of his greatest works, chiefly of mannequin figures.

The mannequin pictures of 1915 fall into two relatively separate categories: those in which the mannequin's head or torso is partially hollowed out; and those in which its surfaces are unbroken. A possible beginning of the first-named group may be found in the small and rather sketchy picture *The Inconsistencies of the Thinker* (page 208), whose title in this exceptional case may have been invented, as he claimed, by André Breton. The torso of the figure has been cut away to reveal an inner paraphernalia of springs and tubes. A comparable, though more authoritative work is the picture often reproduced as *The Astronomer* (page 209), though the back of the canvas is inscribed in the painter's early handwriting as *L'Inquiétude de la mie*. In this picture areas of sky and a torque-like spine are visible through clefts in the mannequin's metallic casing, its overlapping sections suggesting medieval suits of armor.

Both these paintings recall the robots which had been so skillfully manufactured in earlier centuries. In *The Two Sisters* (page 211) and *The Fatal Light* (page 210), however, the robot-like figure is accompanied by a stuffed and sewn mannequin such as de Chirico had already utilized in 1914 in *The Dream of the Poet* and *The Endless Voyage*, inspired in part perhaps by dummies in clothing stores. What a strange head is that in the foreground of *The Two Sisters!* Its eyes are architectural arches, its wig of an absurd yet strangely menacing artificiality. The handling of the wig typifies the economy of pictorial means of which de Chirico was a consummate master during his early career. We may compare it with profit to the treatment of the wig in *The Two Masks* (page 146), an undated work which is usually assigned to the year 1916 but which was almost certainly not painted before 1918 and possibly later. In the latter picture there is evident a debilitating baroque complication of contour, obvious in the wig and eyes of the figure and in the curlicued forms of the foreground still life. *The Two Sisters* strikes at our consciousness with uncanny directness; *The Two Masks* tapers off into contrived elegance. There is a great difference in emotional force in the treatment of the background mannequin in the two pictures. In the former work the mannequin is a quizzical witness to some inexplicable but memorable action; in the latter it becomes merely a theatrical property.

The wig, now reduced to a toupée, recurs in *The Fatal Light*. The hollowed cranium on which it is placed is presumably made of some hard substance which contrasts with the soft, closed surfaces of the accompanying mannequin. Through the hollowed-out head are seen the by now familiar wall and half-concealed train, separated from the head by a brilliantly lighted piazza. At the right the composition is enclosed by architecture and a curious scroll, capped by the rounded epaulet which is among the artist's most enigmatic inventions. The upper area of the picture is enlivened by a bright flag—an exceptionally clear example of de Chirico's inspired sense of plastic order at this stage of his career. The image as a whole is thoroughly fantastic. Yet it conveys a real impression of disquiet and suspense, like a sequence remembered on waking from a troubled dream.

The Philosopher and the Poet (page 63) is dated 1914. Two drawings of the same subject exist: one dated 1913; the other 1915 (page 62). The painting is a puzzling work as to date, since its loose technique contrasts with the firm clarity of the mannequin series as a whole. It seems indeed to be an unfinished picture, probably begun before de Chirico's departure from Paris in 1915, but also possibly revised at a later date. De Chirico's procedure during his first stay in Paris was to paint over a quite precise linear understructure, unlike that which characterizes *The Philosopher and the Poet*. Certainly the picture could not have been finished a year before *The Seer* (page 104), whose 1915 date has never been disputed. In 1914 the mannequin series as a whole was not as formalized in conception as *The Philosopher and the Poet*, whatever its degree of incompletion would suggest. Moreover, the drawing of the subject dated 1913 is an unusually complete and finished work, considering the rough sketches typical of de Chirico's first Paris period (pages 81—85). The second drawing, inscribed "1915," is far more believable as to date. Yet an odd and confusing fact is that the star-shaped symbols appearing on the blackboards in both drawings are not to be found elsewhere in de Chirico's art of 1911–15, though they figure importantly in the painter's illustrations for an edition of Apollinaire's *Calligrammes*, published as late as 1931. There is therefore some reason to think that the subject was re-worked in later years by the artist.*

At any rate, *The Philosopher and the Poet*, whatever its true date and despite its partly transparent head, belongs to the second category of mannequin pictures—those in which the figures are armless, stuffed dummies. The climax of this brief series is reached with *The Seer* (page 104). The picture is the very epitome of the dire, even if warmed by an incalculable poetry of nostalgic mood. The seer is depicted as a motionless, brooding presence, perched with wing-like shoulders on a pedestal and facing a blackboard on which appear an architectural drawing, some cryptic letters, the word "Torino" and the outline of a statue. This is the work of an artist thoroughly convinced of the power of oracles. Indeed de Chirico's faith in divination and the shades of reality is confirmed by an anecdote recounted by André Breton. One night Breton, Louis Aragon and de Chirico were seated at a café in Paris when a flower-boy appeared so suddenly that Aragon asked Breton whether the youth might not be a phantom. De Chirico, his back to the street, had not seen the boy. But on hearing the conversation, he pulled a mirror from his pocket, studied the boy's image in the glass and gravely announced that this was assuredly a phantom.[100]

The setting of *The Seer* appears to be an exterior court or square, bounded in the distance by a toy-like building with curtained doorway somewhat like that seen in *The Enigma of an Autumn Afternoon* of 1910 (page 165). Alfred H. Barr, Jr., has suggested to the writer that this toy-like building may have been inspired by one of the many small, "portable" buildings in Giotto's frescoes. The suggestion seems pertinent in that de Chirico would certainly have seen Giotto's works in the Church of Santa Croce at Florence. The façade of this church was used, drastically transformed and simplified, in *The Enigma of an Autumn Afternoon*, whose building has been compared above to that in *The Seer*. The columned temple in Giotto's *Zacharias in the Temple* in the

---

* As early as 1917, however, Filippo de Pisis in an article, "Carrà e De Chirico," mentions a painting by de Chirico entitled *Il filosofo e il poeta*. The picture is named in a list of de Chirico's most famous and well-documented early works in the de Pisis article, a fact which lends credence to a date for *The Philosopher and the Poet* prior to 1917. Moreover, in 1931 de Chirico described his lithographs for Apollinaire's *Calligrammes* to René Gaffé as follows: "In making these lithographs which you have before you [he told me] I was inspired by memories which go back to the years 1913 and 1914. I had just come to know the poet. I read avidly those verses of his in which there is frequent mention of suns and stars..." (René Gaffé, *Giorgio de Chirico, Le Voyant*, Brussels, Editions la Boétie, 1946, p. 8).

We must therefore not rule out the possibility that *The Philosopher and the Poet* was indeed painted by the artist before his departure for Italy in the summer of 1915 and that its "suns and stars" were revived by de Chirico in 1931 in his illustrations for Apollinaire's *Calligrammes*.

Church of Santa Croce could well have been imaginatively transposed by the artist into the toy-like building in *The Seer*. Yet the ground is covered with wooden planking, as in *The Duo* (page 213) and *The Double Dream of Spring* (page 212). This fact suggests that the scene takes place indoors. Remembering de Chirico's love of enigmas, it may be that he used the flooring to convey a sense of uncertainty, sometimes felt in late pictures in the Caravaggesque tradition, as to whether a given action occurs within a chamber or in the open air.

The superb mannequin figure dominates *The Seer* through its eloquent strength of contour; its only companion is an oblique shadow cast by a statue such as the one presumably of Bottero which appears in *The Enigma of a Day*. The mannequin's color is exceptionally subtle. Its white head is astonishingly luminous, picking up a greenish reflection from the sky at the left and building up to a blinding purity in the center, its foil the intense black of the image on the easel, held aloft by those strange armatures which, during succeeding years at Ferrara, were to play so important a part in de Chirico's iconography.

Had de Chirico at this point become interested in Mannerist art? There is no evidence to prove that this early in his career he admired sixteenth-century Italian painting, though after 1920 his regard for Michelangelo and for such lesser masters as Dosso Dossi helped bring about his return to classicism. But the bulging distortion of the right leg in *The Seer's* mannequin seems a specifically Mannerist device, and perhaps by 1915 he had been attracted by the proto-Mannerism of the late Renaissance, a supposition which is confirmed by the elegant, contrapuntal stance of the two figures in *The Duo* (page 213).

In *The Duo* the needle-sharp focus of *The Seer* is relaxed somewhat and the mood is more poignant. Indeed if the latter is the strongest and most brilliant of the pictures in the 1915 mannequin series, the former is the most moving and tender. The lovers of *The Duo* stand out against their elegiac setting like figures seen through a stereoscope. Behind them a green sky frames a rose tower whose soft color and bland texture recall the frescoes of Piero della Francesca. Beside the mannequins there is an artificial shrub. The plant's artificiality is conveyed with such acuteness that it becomes, like the wig in *The Two Sisters* (page 211), more real than nature itself. *The Duo* as a whole is remarkable for its masterful application of technique to intention, of hand to poetic imagination, of surface communication to those submarine caverns of the mind where the unconscious rolls with the tide, face down.

The Double Dream of Spring (page 212) is a companion piece to *The Seer* and *The Duo*, though now only one of the protagonists is a mannequin, the other the familiar Victorian statue. Both figures seem to have emerged in somnabulism from the shadowed foreground which presumably was the scene of their dreaming. Between them a canvas-within-the-canvas is placed on an easel. Its blue tone is almost identical to the color of the sky, but differentiated from the latter by a subtle greenish overcast. The picture-within-the-picture includes drawings of various components of de Chirico's early iconography—architecture, a train, a flag, a statue, a landscape, a tower, the legs of Ariadne. But the foreshortened cup or jug is a new motif, a rather puzzling one in that its handling suggests the "metaphysical" technique of Carlo Carrà, as de Chirico pointed out disgustedly in authenticating the picture late in 1949.*

In the background of *The Double Dream of Spring*, the scene of the dream itself is reached by a deep, wooden platform. It is a dream of spring and there is no mistaking it. The sudden warmth in which the diminutive figures have come out to walk and stand, the restlessness and relief of winter's end—these are conveyed with a persuasiveness that goes far beyond the limits of traditional realism, and once again we are reminded of the painter's avowed intention to record the emotional impact of imagined experience rather than to document external appearances. His example opened the way for surrealist artists such as Ernst, Tanguy, Magritte, Dali and Delvaux whose debt to de Chirico all have proudly acknowledged. *The Double Dream of Spring's* relationship to Dali's early art is especially clear; the ambiguous tonal affinity between the sky and the canvas-within-the-canvas puts one in mind at once of many pictures by René Magritte.

TWO PAINTINGS OF ARCHITECTURE: 1915

At some point before his departure from Paris in the summer of 1915 de Chirico painted two predominantly architectural subjects: *The Purity of a Dream* (page 215) and *The Joy of Return* (page 214). Only the former picture is dated 1915 and the latter has often been exhibited as a work of 1913. However, the two paintings' tonal and structural similarity suggests that both were completed at about the same time. In both, the composition is organized around a brilliant white central passage—a puff of smoke in *The Joy of Return*, a canvas with the drawing of a tree in *The Purity of a Dream*. Thus the two pictures seem related to *The Double Dream of Spring*, with its central canvas-within-the-canvas, and there is little reason to doubt that 1915 is the correct date for all three works.

---

* *The Double Dream of Spring* was reproduced in *Time* magazine for August 23, 1946, with the comment that de Chirico had just denounced it as a forgery to one of *Time's* reporters after seeing it reproduced in *The Early Chirico*, a copy of which the writer sent the artist as soon as the war ended and the mails to Italy were open. Late in 1949 the writer sent a photograph of the picture to de Chirico through a mutual friend. De Chirico promptly authenticated the picture in writing and declared that he had been misquoted by *Time's* reporter. The provenience of The *Double Dream of Spring* can be traced back to 1919, when Paul Guillaume sold it to M. Level of the Galerie Percier in Paris.

Both *The Purity of a Dream* and *The Joy of Return* are notable for their dense massing of architectural elements, plane behind plane, as though de Chirico once more had been affected, even if obliquely, by the esthetic of early cubism to which he had been exposed repeatedly in Apollinaire's apartment. A comparable massing of architectural forms occurs in *The Torment of the Poet* (page 204), painted the previous year, but the two works just mentioned are characterized by a more vigorous and deep delineation of arches, windows and doors than heretofore. Indeed, the technical procedure of the 1914 paintings of architectural subjects seems now to have been reversed. Whereas in *The Enigma of a Day* (page 189), for example, the arches are defined as shadowed areas on a sunlit façade, now it is light which throws the apertures into relief against a surrounding dark.

It would be interesting to know whether the labyrinthine character and sobriety of tone of *The Purity of a Dream* and *The Joy of Return* reflect in some degree the artist's despair during the early months of the First World War. We should remember, however, that de Chirico now drew upon a fairly wide tonal range from dark to bright. The little still life, *The Playthings of the Prince* (page 202), dated 1915, is as strong in color as *The Evil Genius of a King* (page 99) and treats a corollary subject. At any rate, de Chirico's early career in Paris was now over, his departure for Italy imminent. Within the short space of three years the young Italian painter, living much alone, had achieved an imagery whose influence has been felt to the ends of the civilized world. The essentials of his great early art had all been established. They were to be expanded, rationalized and formalized into an esthetic creed—*pittura metafisica*—during the years immediately following de Chirico's return to Italy in the summer of 1915.

THE RETURN TO ITALY: ARRIVAL IN FERRARA

Summoned home by the Italian military authorities, de Chirico went to Florence for his physical examination in midsummer, 1915, and was assigned to the 27th Infantry Regiment at Ferrara. We do not know the exact date of his arrival in Ferrara, but he speaks in his autobiography of drilling with his fellow-soldiers in humid, July weather. There is no reason to doubt his recollection of what must have been a painful experience, especially since he was apparently suffering again from a chronic enteric disturbance. But he had no fever and since, according to him, fever was the one medical symptom in which the regiment's doctor put any faith, "despite my physical and mental exhaustion, I could not manage to get even one day of rest."[101]

Presently, however, his case came to the attention of a staff major and he was assigned to headquarters as a clerk together with his brother, Andrea (Alberto Savinio), who had apparently accompanied him from France. His mother meanwhile had moved to Ferrara and taken a furnished apartment—an indication of her fanatical, indeed almost frightening, devotion to her two talented sons. Both sons were allowed to sleep and eat at home and "to think just a bit in one's free time about art and the things of the mind which had always been the ultimate goal of our lives."[102] De Chirico began to paint again in his hours of freedom, and one of the first works he completed in Ferrara must have been a portrait of a new friend, Carlo Cirelli (page 216). The portrait is dated October, 1915, and the face of the canvas includes the longest available inscription in the vertical handwriting which the artist used in signing his early paintings and some completed as late as the mid-1920s. The picture itself is rather reminiscent of the Germanic sources which had so interested de Chirico during his youth at Munich. The influence of Franz Stuck is particularly strong, as Dr. Carlo L. Ragghianti has pointed out.[103]

Soon after his arrival in Ferrara de Chirico came to know Filippo de Pisis, then an extremely young man more interested in writing than in painting but already a draftsman of some distinction. Contrary to general belief, de Pisis was not in the Italian Army with de Chirico and Savinio but lived at home in Ferrara with his well-to-do family, having been exempted from military service. His lively and fantastic mind, together with the intimate knowledge of Ferrara which is recorded in his remarkable book, *La Città dalle 100 Meraviglie* (1920), impressed de Chirico greatly. But we must not take seriously de Pisis' claim that he was a founder of the *scuola metafisica*, soon to be discussed. As noted, he was not yet a painter and in 1917, when de Chirico and Carlo Carrà jointly launched the *scuola metafisica*, he was only twenty-one years old, whereas Carrà at thirty-six was a veteran of the entire Futurist campaign and de Chirico at twenty-nine had his brilliant career in Paris behind him.

FERRARA, 1916: THE NEW STILL-LIFE STYLE

Except in the case of dated pictures, it is extremely difficult to know whether the works de Chirico executed in Ferrara were completed in 1916 or 1917. But there are very considerable differences as to iconography and technique between paintings done in these two years and those belonging to the artist's Paris period (1911–15).

To begin with, at some point late in 1915 or early in 1916 de Chirico temporarily abandoned the mannequin theme and returned to still-life subjects. His new still lifes, however, are for the most part arranged in interior settings, whereas those of the previous years in Paris are all placed in the open air, though a few mannequin pictures of 1915 are ambiguous in setting as noted (page 105). It may be, as suggested earlier, that de Chirico's interest in architectural exteriors waned after his return to Italy, that it had been prompted by a nostalgia for his native land which could not be expected to survive his homecoming. At any rate, the writer has never seen an authentic and properly dated work later than 1914 in which architecture is the predominant theme, with still life or mannequins reduced to accessory dramatic roles. Though architecture is an important iconographical element in certain works completed at Ferrara, notably in those pictures of 1917 which include mannequins, it is no longer *the* subject of de Chirico's art. We need only compare the *Troubadour* (page 234) or *The Grand Metaphysician* (page 133) with *The Departure of the Poet* (page 190) to see clearly a reduction of emphasis on architecture *per se*.

At Paris de Chirico's romanticism had centered on public buildings and squares. At Ferrara he turned to an equally intense preoccupation with the evocative atmosphere of rooms. Indeed the open piazza and the small chamber are the two opposite focal points of his metaphysics, the one for a time completely supplanting the other in his art. That he thought of architectural exteriors and interiors as separate emotional stimulants is apparent from his words on Giotto. After describing the latter's sense of "cosmic mystery" in his use of architecture as subject matter, de Chirico goes on to say:

> The square of the sky seen through the window is a secondary drama that interlocks with the drama of people's imagination. When the eye rests on that blue or greenish expanse held in by the square geometry of stone, many anxious questions come to mind. *What might there be, over there? Does that sky overlook an empty sea or a crowded city? Or does it stretch over a wide, free and restless nature, over wooded mountains, dark valleys, plains furrowed by rivers?* ... And the perspectives of buildings rise full of mystery and misgiving, corners conceal secrets, the work of art ceases to be a terse episode, a scene limited by the actions of the figures represented, and it all becomes a cosmic and vital drama which envelops men and constricts them within its spirals, where past and future merge, where the enigmas of existence, sanctified by the breath of art are divested of the entangled fearfulness that man—outside the world of art—imagines, only to assume the eternal, peaceful, consoling aspect of a work of genius.[104]

In an article on Raphael published the same year (1920), when the enthusiasms of his years at Ferrara were still fresh in memory, de Chirico returned to the subject of the magic atmosphere of certain interiors: "Our first impression on looking at any painting by Raphael is one of solidity. This impression fills us with a deeply spiritual well-being, a sort of comforting rhythm—as if we were in a room of great architectural perfection, with large rectangular windows, cut so high that one could behold neither nature nor the works of man but only the sky—solid and wide—and all the sounds of life would be remote and blurred."[105]

High, wide windows, filled by the sky and occasionally by fragments of a distant architecture—these appear in a number of de Chirico's interiors with still life during the year 1916 (pages 223 and 236). But the contents of the interiors is exceedingly odd and once more the painter's article on Raphael throws light on his own predilection for a troubling illogic:

> Returning to the idea of the empty room unexpectedly occupied by people, I think that the metaphysical and strange appearance taken on by the occupants when we first behold

them, is caused by the fact that all our senses and mental faculties, under the shock of surprise, lose the thread of human logic—the logic to which we have been geared since childhood. Or to put the matter in other words, our mental faculties *forget*, lose their meaning, the life around them comes to a stop, and in that halt of the vital rhythm of the universe the figures we see, while they do not change shape materially, appear as ghosts to our eyes.[106]

The objects shown in de Chirico's 1916–17 interiors with still life are strange ghosts indeed! Many of these objects were probably inspired, though imaginatively transformed, by things the artist had actually seen on walks through the city of Ferrara with his new friend, de Pisis. De Chirico himself is explicit on this point. In his autobiography he writes: "The appearance of Ferrara, one of the loveliest cities in Italy, had made a deep impression on me, but what struck me above all and inspired me from the metaphysical point of view in which I was then working, was the appearance of certain interiors in Ferrara, certain window displays, certain shops, certain houses, certain quarters, as for instance the old ghetto where one could find candy and cookies in exceedingly strange and metaphysical shapes."[107]

In Ferrara's shops de Chirico perhaps saw the drawing instruments and armatures which became a principal iconographical motif in his 1916 still lifes, though we should remember that he had used armatures in certain Parisian works of 1914 and 1915. At Ferrara he may also have seen trays of military decorations such as appear in *The War* (page 217). And his autobiographical reference to the ghetto's exotic, edible objects is especially relevant. For as the war mounted in fury de Chirico's nervous instability and accompanying intestinal disturbances became steadily worse. A common symptom of nervous-gastric illnesses is a longing for forbidden delicacies, and there is very likely a direct relationship between de Chirico's poor health and his persistent use of cookies and candies in his still lifes of 1916–17. In contrast to the bananas, artichokes and eggs that appear in earlier works by the artist, these sweets are depicted with extreme and loving precision, recalling the case of the impoverished nineteenth-century Italian painter described in AMW. Stirling's *The Richmond Papers:* "All the pictures which the luckless man painted were of food—a succulent roast chicken, oysters piled up on a plate, sausages nicely browned in a dish—delicacies so realistically portrayed that it made one hungry to contemplate them."[108]

THE STILL LIFES WITH FOREGROUND CIRCLE

It is impossible to decide authoritatively the chronological sequence of the 1916 still lifes completed at Ferrara. Nor can we be positive that de Chirico now tended to complete one series of related pictures before progressing to another, as he had done in Paris in the case of his paintings on the theme of Ariadne's statue. Yet for the sake of convenience certain works may be considered together.

110

For example, the three still lifes—*Death of a Spirit*, *The War* and *The Homesickness of an Engineer* (pages 217–219)—seem to constitute a group in that all three include a circular, geometric form in the foreground. The form, with ruled graphs, occurs at the extreme right in the first two pictures named, in the lower middle area of the third. *The Death of a Spirit* has often been exhibited as a painting of 1915, quite probably because the biscuits shown in it are French rather than Italian and hence would seem to relate to de Chirico's years in Paris (1911–15). But French cookies of this kind are to be found everywhere in Europe and the complex arrangement of the armatures at the left suggests a 1916 date. Contrarily, however, the thin handling of the passages at the right recalls earlier still lifes such as *The Song of Love*, painted at Paris in 1914 (page 77). It may be therefore that the picture was begun either before or soon after the painter's arrival in Ferrara and was completed at a later date. At any rate, *The Death of a Spirit* combines to a unique degree the differing techniques of de Chirico's Parisian and Ferrarese periods.

The most conspicuous technical change that took place in de Chirico's art after his return to Italy was a new preoccupation with texture, accompanied by a heightened richness of color. In works of the artist's early years in Paris, there is no precedent for the almost encrusted surfaces which characterize the painting of the biscuits in *The War*. De Chirico's emphasis on tactile values was to grow steadily more pronounced until it culminated in the opulent handling of the smoked whitefish or herring in *The Sacred Fish* of 1919 (page 155). Moreover, the military ribbons that appear in *The War* are painted in bright and thoroughly Italian colors which constitute a decided change from the muted tones of the majority of the artist's works of 1912–15. Considered as a whole, *The War* poses a curious problem. Could de Chirico at this point have seen the Vorticist pictures of Wyndham Lewis and his associates in London? Probably not, though remembering the close if brief association between advanced British painters and the Italian Futurists, copies of Lewis' magazine, *Blast*, in which his abstractions based on aerial views were published, may have made their way to Ferrara (possibly into the library of de Chirico's new friend, de Pisis?). In any case, *The War* is closer in spirit to Vorticism than to cubism, notably in its from-above perspective, though not in its realism of detail in the painting of the biscuits.

Both *The War* and *The Homesickness of an Engineer* include heavy black shadows which are more abstract in form than ever before in de Chirico's art. Related to them in this regard is the sensuous little picture, *The Language of a Child* (page 218), wherein the foreground, circular motif which also appears in the three still lifes just discussed consists of a fan-like arrangement of playing cards. The lush modeling of *The Language of a Child* suggests a date as late as 1919, but it is here tentatively assigned to 1916 on the basis of its stylistic affinity to other works of the latter year. It remains a puzzling work, perhaps painted by way of respite from the artist's metaphysical program.

De Chirico's own thrice-repeated statement that the picture is probably a forgery is not to be taken seriously.*

THE STILL LIFES WITH MAPS

On strolls through Ferrara de Chirico was probably impressed by the maps which the anxious days of war had brought into new prominence in shop windows. He included such maps in three still-life compositions, of which two are dated 1916 and the third is clearly of the same period. These are *Politics* (page 220), *Evangelical Still Life* (page 221) and a work usually known, perhaps erroneously, as *The Melancholy of Departure* (page 222). The comparatively bland technique of *Politics* suggests that it is the earliest of the three pictures. Even so, its surfaces are more densely manipulated than those in the earlier paintings of Italian squares, not only in terms of impasto but because of the quite intricate linear hatching used to depict the map's topographic contours. And de Chirico's compositional formula has become more daringly asymmetric than during his Paris period: the busy right section of *Politics* is offset at the left by broad, flat areas of color; the picture's off-balance thrust is strengthened by the odd, irregular dimensions of the map's frame.

De Chirico's interest in unorthodox formats for his paintings has been mentioned in passing. There is no more startling indication of this interest than the curious shape of *Evangelical Still Life*, wherein the canvas and stretcher are shifted out of "true," deliberately of course. The painting's oblique slant is repeated in the framed images within the canvas. In the left one of these interior images two Ionic columns are shown against a dark blue ground, the one in normal position, the other inverted. To the right, gray islands are surrounded by a bright green sea, and above them two biscuits are portrayed with that sumptuous detail which is an earmark of de Chirico's post-Paris style. Perhaps it was the actual texture of edibles and the simulated texture of maps which now led the painter to enliven his still-life objects occasionally with speckled, almost neo-impressionist accents of color, as in the dotted armature of *Evangelical Still Life*. Moreover, whereas de Chirico's forms had once been rigidly angular, now they sometimes became curlicued—a Baroque fancifulness playing against a sterner

* To *Time* magazine's reporter, Charles Wertenbaker, in August, 1946 at Rome, de Chirico denounced as "the handiwork of an unskilled copyist" two paintings reproduced in *The Early Chirico—The Language of a Child*, and *The Double Dream of Spring* (see footnote, page 106). The artist has since authenticated the latter painting. In May, 1950, however, he repeated to a friend his suspicions about *The Language of a Child*, saying that it was "so badly painted that one might believe it to be a Braque"! But his technical objections to the picture, while valid as applied to his present-day procedure, are specious when applied to the brilliant art of his early period. In the writer's opinion the picture is authentic, though it might have been painted in 1919 rather than 1916. (See footnote to Foreword for a report on de Chirico's third and latest denial of this picture.)

geometry. If, for instance, we compare the *Melancholy of Departure* with *The Joys and Enigmas of a Strange Hour* (page 180), we see at once how drastic are the differences between the artist's styles of 1914 and of 1916.

THE STILL LIFES WITH AN EYE

Some time during 1916 de Chirico completed three still lifes which have in common the inclusion of an oval form quite obviously based on the human eye. In the picture known as *Metaphysical Interior, I* (page 228) the eye is instantly recognizable; it makes its appearance as a drawn image on a pyramidal structure in the background, behind a marbleized box or platform of extremely odd dimensions, while at the right there is the by-now familiar congestion of armatures.

In *The Jewish Angel* (page 224) and *The Greetings of a Distant Friend* (page 225), the eye-like form is more abstract and is depicted on a tacked bit of paper with bent corner. The first of these two pictures holds a unique place in the art of de Chirico's Ferrarese period. To begin with, the unusually broad background areas are painted a uniform, light gray and are broken by symmetrically arranged armatures—so common in the painter's canvases of this period. Some of the forms comprising the central structure or "figure" are again curvilinear, almost Baroque. Yet in this authentic example of de Chirico's esthetic procedure after his return to Italy, these forms are crisply defined and are balanced skillfully against more geometric elements. The picture may be compared with profit to those later works, produced in Paris in the mid-1920s, when de Chirico under surrealist prodding was attempting to revive his metaphysical style and when uncertainty of contour became a conspicuous indication of his decline as an artist.

THE "CLAUSTROPHOBIC" INTERIORS

Did the fact that de Chirico was now obliged to spend much of his time in the military hospital of Ferrara have an effect on his art? It seems likely that this was indeed the case and that his rising nervous instability, as the tragedy of the war assumed greater proportions, is reflected in several still lifes of this time for which the word "claustrophobic" does not seem too strong. These still lifes are: *The Regret, The Revolt of the Sage* and *The Faithful Servitor* (pages 226, 227, 223). In all three paintings, and particularly in the first two named, there is a new emphasis on forms descending from the top of the picture space or crowding in from its sides, as though the artist felt abnormally oppressed by his experiences in the hospital, to which more specific reference will be made presently. For now suffice it to say that de Chirico was apparently exempted from active military service for neuropsychiatric reasons and that, as the war became more and more ferocious and deadly, his depression of mind grew steadily more acute.

Mention has been made in passing of a possible symbolic significance for the edible objects which appear so often in de Chirico's still lifes of the Ferrarese period; such objects may also have represented in his distraught mind the delicacies of civilian life. And in *The Regret, The Revolt of the Sage* and, above all, *The Faithful Servitor*, these objects assume a new luxuriousness of tone and texture, as if the painter's longing for the amenities of normal existence had become especially deep. A detailed analysis of de Chirico's iconography from the psychiatric viewpoint is, of course, the province of professionals in the medical field. But we should always keep in mind the fact that from early youth the artist had suffered from melancholia, verging quite likely on psychic disturbance. His friends (and enemies) seem to have been aware of this always, and it is significant that André Billy, speaking of Apollinaire's reaction to de Chirico's pictures, applied to these works the phrase "hypochondriacal dislocation."[109]

THE RETURN TO DEEP PERSPECTIVE

At some point in 1916—and probably late—de Chirico once again began to concern himself with far perspective as an emotive device. Whereas the still lifes we have been discussing are in varying degrees notable for their foreground congestion of forms, a picture such as *The Gentle Afternoon* (page 229) revives the painter's earlier system of projecting objects against an infinity of space, in this instance presumably comprising a vast outdoor platform. And in other paintings like the *Metaphysical Interior with Large Building* (page 230) and its companion piece, *Metaphysical Interior with Small Building* (page 228), though clearly their setting is that of an enclosed room, a far, exterior distance is suggested by the inclusion in each of a framed painting-within-the-painting. Neither picture has the sumptuous textural passages to be found in what have been described as the "claustrophobic" still lifes. But both are notable for their clear brilliance of color. Their evident relationship to certain "metaphysical" interiors of 1917 suggests that they were executed late the previous year.

One of the most brilliant of de Chirico's Ferrarese works is entitled *The Amusements of a Young Girl* (page 231). There is little precedent in de Chirico's art for the Courbet-like solidity of the modeling of the leather glove, and not until 1919, with *The Sacred Fish* (page 155), did the artist's technique become so thoroughly sensuous. Yet there is every other reason to believe that the picture was finished at Ferrara in 1916 or 1917, probably the former. The building in the background is obviously Ferrara's famed red Castello Estense (page 60); the box of matches in the foreground is labelled "Ferrara"; the handling of the architecture, the flooring and the board on which the glove is pinned indicates a 1916 or 1917 date. Certainly the picture was completed before the end of the war and long before de Chirico's growing interest in

Courbet prompted him to write a monograph on the French master (published in 1925). At any rate, *The Amusements of a Young Girl* is one of the handsomest and most condensed of all the painter's many still-life compositions.

1917: THE ARRIVAL OF CARLO CARRÀ AND THE FOUNDING OF THE SCUOLA METAFISICA

In January, 1917, Carlo Carrà, one of the five original artist-members of the Futurist movement, arrived in Ferrara. Like de Chirico he was in the Italian Army, and both artists were assigned to a convalescent hospital (it had been a convent before the war) a few kilometres outside the city. The two men became friends and from their association evolved the *scuola metafisica* (the metaphysical school), whose tenets were in essence a rationalization of the art de Chirico had been creating since his arrival in Paris in 1911.

Both de Chirico and Carrà were allowed to paint in the hospital. But the legend that they offered their pictures to the medical officers as proof of their unfitness for active duty is almost certainly untrue. What we do know is that Carrà had brought with him to the barracks at Ferrara his book of Futurist sketches of war scenes. In his own words, "Upon my arrival at Pieve di Cento I happened to make a present of my book, *Guerra-Pittura*, to the captain of the Company. Evidently he was upset by it and he began to take it out on me and to harass me in every way imaginable." [110] Quite likely from this incident arose the legend that the metaphysical paintings of Carrà and de Chirico were considered proof of their mental and nervous instability by the military authorities. But de Chirico had been on the inactive list since his arrival in Ferrara a year and a half earlier, and there is no reason to believe that either his paintings or Carrà's were studied as clinical evidence by the army doctors, though Carrà's book of Futurist sketches may well have irritated his captain to the point of persecuting the artist. But that is apparently all there is to the legend that de Chirico's pictures were considered the work of a madman by his superiors in the Italian Army. The legend for many years was fostered by the surrealists, who regarded insanity with an awe comparable to that felt by Romantics of a hundred years earlier like Géricault, and who therefore delighted in the idea that de Chirico's art, to which they owed so much, had once been labelled mad.

But by what route did Carrà's painting reach a point of close relationship to that of de Chirico? Carrà, to repeat, had been one of the five original artist-members of the Futurist movement. By 1915, however, the founding quintet of Futurist art, with the exception of Balla, had begun to desert the movement, though new recruits like Ottone Rosai and Mario Sironi put in a brief appearance. In 1916 Carrà published in *La Voce* articles in praise of Giotto and Uccello and first pondered that return to native tradition which was to leave revolutionary experiment behind and culminate in the deliberately reactionary *Novecento* movement of the 1920s. The same year he painted several primitivist works, among them the *Antigrazioso* and the *Tramantici*, in which the Futurist esthetic was abandoned in favor of a direct naïveté of expression based on the great mid-fifteenth-century Italian masters and on self-taught moderns like the Douanier Rousseau, whose quality Carrà recognized at an early date and later described in his book, *Pittura Metafisica* (1919). Though Carrà continued to sign some of his pictures "C. D. Carrà—Futurista" as late as 1917, by the end of 1915 he was in search of a stylistic and idiomatic substitute in contemporary terms for the emotional intensity of the old masters and the modern primitives. He found a solution very soon after his arrival in Ferrara—the enigmatic dislocations of surface reality proposed by de Chirico's art.

Early in 1917 Carrà's imagery began to reflect the influence of de Chirico. Considerable confusion has arisen, however, due to the fact that certain metaphysical paintings by Carrà are dated 1916—that is, prior to his arrival in Ferrara and before he knew de Chirico or his work. The explanation probably lies in the fact that Carrà then and later often re-worked his canvases over a long period of time. *The Drunken Gentleman* (page 121), for example, may have been begun in 1916 (its inscribed date) as quite a different picture, drastically repainted after the meeting with de Chirico at Ferrara. The picture's croquet stake appears in several of the latter's still lifes of 1917, and there can be no question that de Chirico was the inventive spirit in the *scuola metafisica*.

This is not to say, however, that Carrà did not bring to metaphysical painting his own qualities as an artist. If in matters of iconography his Ferrarese works are heavily indebted to de Chirico, they have nevertheless their own separate technical virtues, particularly as to the use of heavily encrusted impasto. There are in existence only about twelve of these works in all. They lack the uncanny impact of de Chirico's paintings of 1916–17, being soft, lush and tender, whereas de Chirico's art is grave and disquieting.

Contrary to widespread belief, the *scuola metafisica* lasted only a very brief time as the joint program of de Chirico and Carrà. In the spring of 1917, a few months after his arrival at Ferrara, Carrà was given convalescent leave by the Army and went to Milan, where he held an exhibition of his Futurist and metaphysical works at the Chini Gallery. De Chirico, on the contrary, remained at Ferrara until after the end of the war and not until early 1919 was he able to hold an exhibition of his recent painting at Bragaglia's Gallery in Rome. In his autobiography the artist bitterly accuses Carrà of having tried to take credit for the invention of metaphysical painting:

Having later obtained a long convalescent leave, Carlo Carrà hastened back to Milan, taking with him all the "metaphysical" pictures he had painted in the hospital at Ferrara. In Milan he promptly organized a show of these paintings, hoping to establish himself as the single and unique inventor of metaphysical painting, so that I would at most appear as an obscure and modest imitator. Of course all these manoeuvres were incredibly ingenuous, since it was common knowledge that I had painted metaphysical pictures in Paris and that they had been exhibited, reproduced and bought.[111]

De Chirico's accusation seems just if over-violent. In any case, the breach between himself and Carrà widened when, in 1919, Carrà published his book, *Pittura Metafisica*, thus once again seeming to claim to have been the founder rather than the chief disciple of the metaphysical school. The book's title is misleading in that only one chapter deals directly with the premise of the *scuola metafisica*, though interspersed throughout the text are many comments and criticisms pertinent to an understanding of the school's program.

De Chirico reviewed Carrà's book adversely in *Il Convegno* in 1920 and the friendship between the two painters came to an end. But their movement began to be known internationally only after their active collaboration was over. In 1919 Mario Broglio launched his magazine, *Valori Plastici*, which published pictures and articles by both de Chirico and Carrà. The magazine's circulation was small, but it reached an important professional audience in Europe. Moreover, Broglio organized an art gallery in Rome, also called Valori Plastici, and under this same title sent out traveling exhibitions of metaphysical painting, notably to Germany, where de Chirico's pictures made an immense impression on Max Ernst and other members of the Dada group.

Both de Chirico and Carrà continued to produce *pittura metafisica* for several years after their quarrel. Carrà's last work in this vein was *The Engineer's Mistress* of 1921, while de Chirico, as we shall have reason to note, reverted to his metaphysical style at intervals until the late 1920s.

OTHER ASSOCIATES OF THE METAPHYSICAL SCHOOL

With de Chirico and Carrà at Ferrara was the former's brother, Alberto Savinio, who died in 1953, whose part in the inspiration of de Chirico's mannequin theme has already been mentioned (page 97). Savinio's contribution to the *scuola metafisica* at Ferrara is difficult to make precise. He was not at that time the active painter he was to become in later years. But he was an extremely cultivated man, talented in the fields of music and literature (in Paris he had been a Futurist composer, noted for the extreme violence with which he played his own compositions on the piano). Savinio may well have acted as a sort of cultural mentor for the *scuola metafisica* until, presumably at some point in 1917, he was transferred by the Italian Army to Macedonia. He is said to have abandoned musical composition in the spring of 1915, though he returned to it in later years, creating scores for the ballet. He was a prolific writer throughout his career, and in the later 1920s began to paint pictures which continued the more fantastic aspects of his brother's metaphysical school.

The painter, Filippo de Pisis, was also at Ferrara during the war years, as already noted. But we can not take seriously de Pisis' claim that he was an active painter in the war-time *scuola metafisica*. His few metaphysical pictures (see page 124) were all almost certainly completed around 1925, despite earlier dates sometimes given them by the artist. Yet there is little doubt that de Pisis' passion for exotic and fantastic objects was an important factor in the evolution of the metaphysical still life. In all probability it was he who guided de Chirico through the streets of the ghetto at Ferrara. De Pisis' room in his family's house seems to have impressed de Chirico, who describes the room as follows: "In Ferrara in his father's house [de Pisis] lived in a strange room full of bizarre and incongruous objects: stuffed birds, strangely shaped *inguastade*, decanters, medicine bottles, assorted crockery and books so old that they crumbled at the first touch. He lived in this sort of wizard's workshop, a true surrealist *ante litteram*." [112]

The only other artist who can properly be said to have belonged, if briefly, to the *scuola metafisica*, is Giorgio Morandi, now revered by many Italian critics and connoisseurs as their finest living painter. But Morandi was never in Ferrara; indeed to this day he has seldom left his native Bologna. He had apparently met Carrà at a Futurist gathering in 1912 at Bologna and, despite his isolation in a relatively provincial city, was aware of advanced developments in contemporary art. Certain Morandi landscapes of 1912, for example, show the influence of Cézanne and the cubists. By 1918 he had seen reproductions of Carrà's metaphysical pictures, and from that year until 1920 his paintings revealed definite affinities with the esthetic of the *scuola metafisica*. These affinities, however, were mainly iconographic. In technique and more especially in underlying premise his pictures parallel those of the Parisian Purists—Ozenfant and Le Corbusier, whose book, *Après le cubisme,* appeared in 1918 and probably was seen by Morandi. His works of 1918–20 are deeply modeled in contrast to the flat style of his French colleagues in Purism. But they are equally concerned with formal as opposed to psychological or philosophical values. And when in 1918 Morandi turned to the mannequin theme—a consistent favorite of both de Chirico and Carrà—he did so primarily, one assumes, because the rounded, smooth contours of the mannequins could supply an appealing plastic counterfoil to the still-life elements in his art, chiefly bottles and tables at that period. If we compare his mannequin pictures with those of de Chirico, and, to a lesser degree, of Carrà, we see that his aim was not to create a psychologically disturbing imagery, but to arrive at a pristine compositional order. His place in the *scuola metafisica* was peripheral at most, though his paintings were published with those of de Chirico and Carrà in *Valori Plastici.* Morandi did not meet de Chirico personally until after the war. He was never an intimate friend of either that artist or Carrà and never discussed with them the tenets of the *scuola metafisica*.

Among Italian contemporaries of de Chirico and Carrà the two painters, Ardengo Soffici and Mario Sironi (page 124), were for a brief interval right after the war affected by the metaphysical school's premise and, especially, its iconography. But neither painter played an active part in the school's short existence.

THE THEORIES OF THE SCUOLA METAFISICA

The metaphysical school was never in any sense an extensive, formal movement in art as cubism had been, nor did its few members engage in the polemical activities which had engrossed the Futurists. Instead, as Alberto Savinio once told the writer, the *scuola metafisica* represented a state of mind common to a very small group of painters for whom the plastic reappraisal of reality—cubism—was less important than a reallocation of reality's component parts, each more or less realistically depicted and sometimes combined with overt fantasies.

De Chirico's views on the need for a drastic rejection of the tangible world have been discussed in relation to his earlier career in Paris. His views are echoed in the pages of Carrà's book, *Pittura Metafisica,* as when the latter artist writes: "We must not forget, however, that if we do understand art, this is the result of another process of the mind which has nothing to do with abandoning oneself to the currents of sensation; therefore it follows that we instinctively carry out an operation of knowledge preceding knowledge itself—this operation is nowadays called intuition, and here we move toward the metaphysical..."[113] And again: "The creative spirit gropes somewhat like a sleepwalker in the fields of the absolute, but our trained sensibility comes into play when we are confronted with an art that is susceptible to multiple interpretations."[114] And still further: "We do not like a confusion of geometries; on the contrary, we like to give our canvases the expression of a simple, mysterious, plastic reality, like a fact of Nature."[115]

In brief, de Chirico and Carrà wished to propose a new reality whose impact would depend in part on a certain mystery of incongruity. By wrenching objects—and frequently commonplace ones, like biscuits, candies, toys, sticks and drawing instruments—out of their normal context, they aspired to suggest a counter-reality which would communicate directly with our subconscious minds. And however numerous the differences between their program and that later evolved by the surrealists (particularly as to the use of Freudian symbols), there can be no doubt that their metaphysical works foretold the art of surrealism to an important degree, a fact of which many leading surrealists were fully aware.

DE CHIRICO AND CARRÀ AS METAPHYSICAL PAINTERS

Though the association between de Chirico and Carrà was of very brief duration, it is important to keep in mind the differences between them as artists. De Chirico, as we have seen, had been nourished by Germanic and primarily philosophic sources, while Carrà, after he had begun to turn away from Futurism's violent experiments, had become immersed in the great Italian tradition of painting. At intervals Carrà revived certain technical elements of his Futurist style, as in his *Penelope* of 1917 (page 123). He apparently hoped for a time to strike an equation between what he described as the two basic concerns of art—movement and static calm. This ambition, best exemplified by *The Cavalier of the West*, proved insuperably difficult, and finally the monumental authority of his favorite medieval and Renaissance masters won out in his mind over Futurism's kinetics. By the close of 1915, his autobiography states, "I can affirm that I had the strongest desire to identify my painting with history and especially with the history of Italian art." [116]

Carrà's deep respect for the plastic solutions of his great predecessors in Italian art is worth noting, for this was the foundation of his approach to metaphysical painting at Ferrara. De Chirico, on the contrary, praised Max Klinger in the following, opposite terms: "the pictorial question did not matter, because his entire creation was based on the enormous possibilities of his exceptional mind—the mind of a poet, philosopher, observer, dreamer and psychologist." [117] And while Carrà particularly admired Giotto, Piero della Francesca and Uccello, de Chirico, when finally he, too, began to be nourished by the Italian tradition in art, turned to Raphael, Michelangelo and Dosso Dossi—an essentially different group of artists from those preferred by Carrà.

The only shared esthetic experience of the two leaders of the *scuola metafisica* was their first hand knowledge of advanced developments in twentieth-century Parisian art. As a Futurist Carrà had naturally been influenced by the cubists, while certain de Chirico paintings suggest that he may also have been impressed by the abstract artists whose ardent champion was his friend, Guillaume Apollinaire. But by 1917 or soon thereafter, Carrà's interest focussed not only on the Douanier Rousseau but on a leading French traditionalist, André Derain. He published a monograph on the latter painter in 1921. But de Chirico, returned to Italy, took at most a minor interest in the School of Paris. To its outstanding figures he almost certainly preferred as artists Böcklin, Klinger, Courbet and, after the First World War, Michelangelo, Raphael and Dosso Dossi.

DE CHIRICO'S MANNEQUIN PAINTINGS: FERRARA, 1916-17

At Ferrara de Chirico returned to the mannequin theme which had engrossed him in Paris before his departure for Italy. He painted two versions of *Hector and Andromache* (pages 232 and 233); the first, which the writer has never seen and which has disappeared in Germany, was presumably executed in 1916; the second is dated 1917. In the latter year he also completed the *Troubadour* (page 234). In the writer's opinion these are the only three paintings of mannequins which may definitely be assigned to

Carrà: *The Drunken Gentleman*, 1916(?). Oil on canvas, 23⁵/₈ x 17¹/₂".
Collection Carlo Frua de Angeli, Milan

Carrà: *The Enchanted Room*, 1917. Oil on canvas, 26 x 20³/₄". Collection
Emilio Jesi, Milan

Carrà: *Penelope*, 1917. Oil on canvas, 38 × 21³/₄″. Collection
Carlo Frua de Angeli, Milan

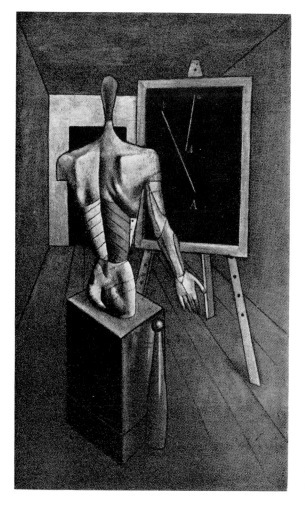

Carrà: *Solitude*, 1917. Oil on canvas, 28³/₄ × 17³/₄″
Collection Sigfried Giedion, Zurich

Sironi: *Mannequin*, Oil on canvas, 21 x 13".
Collection Riccardo Jucker, Milan

De Pisis: *The "Mad Poet" of Giorgio de Chirico*, 1919(?).
Collection Carlo Cardazzo, Venice

Morandi: *Mannequin on a Round Table*, 1918. Oil on canvas, 19¹/₄ × 23¹/₄". Collection Riccardo Jucker, Milan

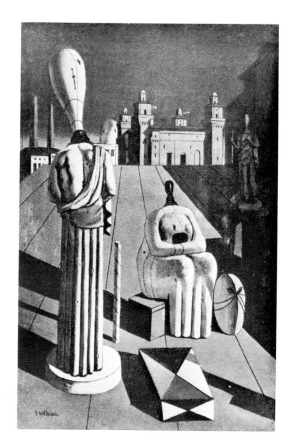

De Chirico: *The Disquieting Muses*, 1917. Oil on canvas,
38¼ x 26". The Gianni Mattioli Foundation,
Milan. Feroldi collection. Reproduced in color, page 135

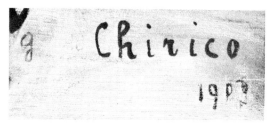

Signature and date of de Chirico's *The Transformed
Dream*, above, and of *Self Portrait*, left. Infra-red
photographs by Charles Uht

De Chirico: *The Disquieting Muses*, 1924. Oil on canvas. Collection Mrs. Jonathan Tichenor, New York

De Chirico: *The Disquieting Muses*, c. 1947(?). Oil on canvas. Collection Arturo Deana, Venice

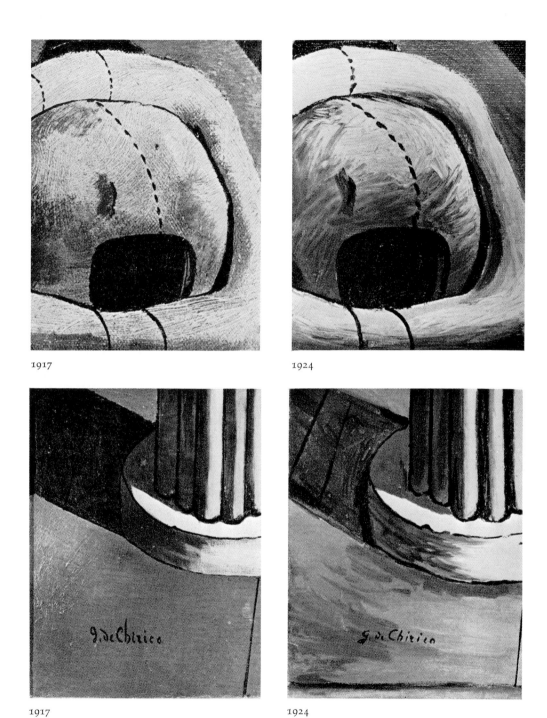

1917

1924

1917

1924

Details of two paintings by de Chirico: *The Disquieting Muses* of 1917 and *The Disquieting Muses* of 1924. Charles Uht photographs the Ferrarese period if we exclude *The Grand Metaphysician* (page 133) and *The Disquieting Muses* (page 135) in which the figures are not, strictly speaking, mannequins.

Confusion has arisen, however, due to the fact that de Chirico has painted a number of canvases with Hector and Andromache, represented by mannequins, as their subject. Some of these pictures are later variants by the artist himself, dating perhaps from as early as 1918 (page 143) and continuing through the 1920s, by which time unmistakable changes in his technique had taken place. The *Hector and Andromache* of 1924 (page 143) is a case in point. Its iridescent brushwork and loose contours suggest that de Chirico had finally become interested in such masters as Rubens and Delacroix and had become absorbed in problems of technical virtuosity on which, in the puritanical leanness of his earlier career, he had turned his back. The artist has also executed several paintings of two mannequins, entitled *Hector and Andromache*, whose inscribed dates are open to doubt. And outright forgeries by other hands have often appeared on the market, here and abroad. Indeed, perhaps no single subject in de Chirico's early art has been so widely copied and abused by himself and others.

The Troubadour and the *Hector and Andromache* of 1917 differ from their 1915 prototypes in two important respects. To begin with, the mannequin figures are more mannered and elegant in contour and stance, as though the painter while at Ferrara had turned his attention to the sixteenth-century, pre-Baroque tradition in Italian art. In both pictures the mannequins are held erect by and cloaked in still-life elements typical of de Chirico's Ferrarese period. These elements include elaborate armatures and triangular forms, now sometimes speckled in surface.

The two paintings under discussion are brighter and flatter in color than *The Seer* of 1915 (page 104), and they lack the latter picture's atmosphere of poignant foreboding. But they are handsome and accomplished works of art. If *Hector and Andromache* seems almost theatrical by comparison with *The Seer*, it is nevertheless a memorable image whose originality later copies by the artist or by forgers have done nothing to spoil. It may profitably be compared with *The Duo* of 1915 (page 213) and with the *Hector and Andromache* of 1924 (page 143). The comparison makes plain de Chirico's gradual evolution from a possessed romantic to a Baroque classicist, from a "primitive" (in the loose sense of the term) to a sobered technician. In the process the artist's emotional force, springing from personal chimera, was diluted by a preoccupation with recondite technical matters—a preoccupation amounting to the obsession recorded in his book, *Piccolo Trattato di Tecnica Pittorica* (Milan, 1928).

THE 1917 STILL LIFES

The head of what appears to be a tailor's dummy or mannequin is found in the beguiling little *Metaphysical Interior* (page 236) along with cookies mounted on a board, armatures and a new and unique object in de Chirico's still-life art—a fishing bobbin. The picture's composition is extremely complex but nonetheless convincing and the painting of the bobbin and biscuits typifies the artist's growing richness of color and modeling. He had now become to a greater extent than ever before a sensuous painter; the odd, mineral-like forms at the right of a second *Metaphysical Interior* (page 235) are especially notable for their dextrous impasto and highlighting.

In two paintings of 1917, foreground still lifes are combined with background architecture, as in certain works of de Chirico's earlier career in Paris. These are the *Metaphysical Interior with Biscuit and Cigarette Holder* (page 236) and *Evangelical Still Life* (page 237). (The titles are probably not the ones originally given by the artist, and the second picture is not to be confused with the painting of 1916 reproduced on page 221.) Both are unique in certain respects. In the former picture a framed picture of a large-scale building appears within an interior room and, at the right, architecture is again seen through an open window. The dislocation of surface reality is intense, the juxtaposition of traditionally unrelated still-life objects wry in the extreme. And in the painting of the cigarette holder, with its cracks and scars, we see de Chirico moving toward that more solid realism of detail which was to characterize certain pictures of 1919.

The *Evangelical Still Life's* background architecture is singularly prophetic of the modern, skyscraper buildings which came into vogue in New York City and elsewhere some years later. One assumes that the architecture was pure invention on de Chirico's part—a radiant foil to the diminutive mannequin figure and to the strange forms, including a yellow chevron on blue ground, which appear in the boxed or framed picture-within-the-picture at the right of the composition. The painting's relative flatness of texture is relieved diagonally by the richly handled biscuits at the lower left and the dappled armatures at the upper right. This is an evocative image, and no one but de Chirico, with his inspired sense of fantasy, could possibly have created it.

The inscribed date of *Evangelical Still Life* is September, 1917. Four months earlier de Chirico had completed *The Scholar's Playthings* (page 238), its anatomical chart presumably inspired by apothecaries' displays which the artist had seen on his strolls through Ferrara. The handling of space in this disturbing picture is unusually subtle. It depends on tonal as well as linear extensions of perspective, suggesting once more that de Chirico had profited from the lessons of the Parisian cubists. In the background flat planes of color are juxtaposed to define a receding distance which reaches its far-thest point in the little green square near the center of a framed, dark ground. The painting of the anatomical charts is both literal and fine. To the left of the charts, affixed to one of those odd, box-like forms of which de Chirico was fond, are two

OPPOSITE: *Grand Metaphysical Interior*, 1917. 37 x 27". Private collection, New Canaan, Connecticut

130

triangles and a picture of a deserted factory. Behind the box is found the striped stick (a croquet stick?) which Carrà also included in *The Drunken Gentleman* (page 121), a picture probably revised after that painter had seen de Chirico's metaphysical works.

The climax of de Chirico's 1917 still-life series is reached in the *Grand Metaphysical Interior* (page 131), one of the most beautiful pictures in color of his entire early career. To the right are hung what seem to be window shades, like those commonly found in Neapolitan houses and shop fronts. At the left, as a framed picture-within-the-picture, is a beguiling landscape with winding road, fountain and small resort hotel and beyond the hotel a lake or harbor bathed in luminous sunlight. The realism of the scene is extreme, as though de Chirico had already begun to admire Courbet about whose art he was later to write an enthusiastic monograph. As in the case of his regard for Böcklin, de Chirico may well have made technical use of Courbet's example some years before he decided to write about the latter master. In any case, the richly painted landscape with hotel is a long cry from the arid impasto of the artist's architectural scenes of 1913–14. De Chirico's new emphasis on realistic modeling is nowhere better exemplified than in the handling of the crusted brioches within their boxed frame. The *Grand Metaphysical Interior* proposes an unforgettable counterplay between realism of detail and fantasy of over-all invention.

THE GRAND METAPHYSICIAN AND THE DISQUIETING MUSES

In 1917 de Chirico completed *The Grand Metaphysician* (opposite), one of his major works of which several later versions exist, notably one erroneously dated 1916 and another correctly dated 1925 (both page 145) and painted at a time when the painter was attempting to revive his metaphysical style under pressure from the surrealists. A comparison of the three pictures tells us a great deal about the technical and iconographical changes which took place in de Chirico's art after his departure from Ferrara in the winter of 1918–19, when he was demobilized from the Army. The original painting is both monumental and restrained; its evocation of the poetic atmosphere of a vast piazza is deeply moving. And the metaphysician's figure is composed of relatively simple, mostly angular forms, whereas in the later versions it becomes a complicated heap of strange bric-a-brac, over-contrived and lacking in emotional impact. As he gained in technical virtuosity after his years at Ferrara, de Chirico's vision softened, with exceptions later to be noted. He no longer worked for the most part like one possessed but with calculated interest in surface effects, sometimes verging on naturalism. The difference in lighting in the 1917 and 1925 versions of *The Grand Metaphysician* is a case in point. The dreamlike luminosity of the former picture is

OPPOSITE: *The Grand Metaphysician,* 1917. 41¼ x 27½". Collection Philip L. Goodwin, New York

replaced in the latter by recognizable daylight coming from a sky with banal, neo-classic clouds, and the atmospheric illusion of suspense and omen is lost. After the war de Chirico's inspiration, so largely oneiric in source, began to wane, though it revived at intervals as when, in 1919, he painted *The Sacred Fish* (page 155).

Also dating from 1917 is what may well be the greatest painting of de Chirico's entire career—*The Disquieting Muses* (opposite). Of this work, also, at least two other versions exist. The first of these (page 127) was painted by the artist for Paul Eluard in 1924, after Giorgio Castelfranco, who then owned the original version, had refused to sell the latter except for a high price. Fortunately the correspondence arranging the 1924 commission has survived, so that there can be no doubt whatever as to its correct date.*

The third version of *The Disquieting Muses* (page 127) poses a more difficult problem. The picture is dated 1918 and its owner, a Venetian collector, has a letter from de Chirico confirming the inscribed date and stating that this is the finest and most definitive of the three versions. But it seems odd that the existence of a 1918 version was not mentioned by de Chirico in writing to the Eluards in 1924. Moreover, it is curious that until its appearance in Venice after World War II, the picture was unknown to such Italian authorities on de Chirico's early career as Giorgio Castelfranco and Anton Giulio Bragaglia (who gave the artist his first one-man exhibition in Italy at Rome in 1919). And finally, when the writer first saw the painting in Venice in 1948, it looked freshly painted, its surfaces bright and "unsettled," as though it had come off the easel only a short time before. The picture is nevertheless a handsome work, more skillfully executed than the 1924 replica whose sloppiness by comparison with the original 1917 version is revealed by macrophotographs (page 128).

To return to the subject of the first *Disquieting Muses*, its background consists of a fairly literal replica of the façade of the Castello Estense at Ferrara (page 60), a

---

* On February 23, 1924, de Chirico wrote from Rome to Paul Eluard's wife (now Mme Gala Dali) as follows: "As soon as I received your amiable letter I wrote to my friend in Florence, M. Castelfranco, the owner of *The Disquieting Muses*, urging him to let you have the picture at the price of 1,200 francs which you propose. He might raise some objection because of the rate of exchange . . . but be assured, Madame, that I will do everything possible so that you can have this painting at the price you propose to me."

On March 10, 1924, he again wrote Mme Eluard: "Here is the problem: my friend in Florence, despite my urging, does not wish to sell the *Muses* for less than 3,500 Italian lire; as to *The Sacred Fish*, it belongs to M. Broglio, who I believe asks 5,000 Italian lire for it. If you wish exact replicas of these two paintings I can make them for you for 1,000 Italian lire each. These replicas will have no other fault than that of being executed in a more beautiful medium and with a more knowledgeable technique. I hope, dear Madame, to have a reply soon . . ."

According to the late Paul Eluard the replica of the *Muses* was ordered promptly and completed that same year (1924). So far as is known, the replica of *The Sacred Fish* was never made, certainly not for the Eluards at this date.

OPPOSITE: *The Disquieting Muses*, 1917. 38¼ x 26". The Gianni Mattioli Foundation, Milan. Feroldi Collection

majestic red palace which had appeared in de Chirico's *The Amusements of a Young Girl* (page 231). The Castello Estense in the *Muses* is flanked by a factory with red chimneys and the portico of a dark building. The piazza leading to the background architecture is incalculably deep and seems to consist of wide, wooden planking. On the piazza are placed two of the most haunting of the artist's fantastic figures—sculptured mannequins, one of which has placed its head beside the blue box on which it sits. The figures are accompanied by the bizarre bric-a-brac of the dream world they inhabit, including a striped stick and a rectangular box ruled into triangles of contrasting colors. — To quote from the writer's description of the picture in *Twentieth-Century Italian Art:* [118]

Perhaps more forcefully than any other work of de Chirico's career the *Muses* illustrates the ambivalent, "metaphysical" nature of his early art. The picture attracts and repels, beguiles and frightens, conveys a warm nostalgic aura but at the same time suggests an impending catastrophe. There is no action; the piazza is still; the figures wait. What will happen? There is no answer, for this picture is the exact opposite of those seventeenth-century paintings of *banditti* in which a specific, disastrous outcome is foretold. De Chirico's image—his early art as a whole—appeals directly to the counter-logic of the subconscious, to those swamp-like regions at the edge of the mind where ecstasies bloom white and the roots of fear are cypress-black and deep.

1918: THE END OF THE WAR; DE CHIRICO'S DEPARTURE FROM FERRARA

The year 1917 was the last consistently great year of de Chirico's early period. At least that is the theory widely publicized by the artist's most effective champions (and disparagers, as to his later works)—the surrealists. And there is little reason to dispute the surrealists' claim, though it is an ironical fact that one of the most influential pictures in the formation of their esthetic or counter-esthetic was *The Sacred Fish* (page 155), completed by de Chirico in 1919, two years after his supposed demise as a creative figure.

But what paintings and how many did de Chirico produce during 1918, before his departure from Ferrara very late in the year? Quite a few drawings dated 1918 have appeared here and abroad since the recent war; they continue to show the technical precision and careful use of modeling to which the artist had turned in 1917. There is in fact little difference in spirit or execution between the climactic drawing of 1917, entitled *Solitude* (page 89), and a 1918 drawing of a seated mannequin (page 86). It was in painting that de Chirico began to change his style and technique during the latter year.

The 1918 picture, *Metaphysical Interior with Waterfall* (page 239) is a case in point. If we compare the boxed landscape of the picture-within-the-picture with that in the *Grand Metaphysical Interior* of the year before, we see that de Chirico had become

De Chirico: *Self Portrait*, 1919. Oil on canvas, 24⁷/₈ × 20".
Private collection, Italy

De Chirico: *Portrait of the Artist with His Mother*, 1919.
Oil on canvas, 31 × 21¹/₂". Collection Edward James, London

De Chirico: *The Return of the Prodigal*, 1919.
Oil on canvas, 32 × 35⅝". Collection Sportano,
Milan

De Chirico: Copy of Michelangelo's *Holy Family*
(Uffizi Gallery, Florence), 1920. L'Obelisco
Gallery, Rome

De Chirico: *Roman Villa*, 1922. Tempera, 40×30". Collection G. Bruno Pagliai, Mexico City

OPPOSITE ABOVE: De Chirico: *The Departure of the Argonauts*, 1922.
Tempera, $21^5/_8$ x $29^1/_4$". Collection Oreste Caciabue, Milan

OPPOSITE BELOW: De Chirico: *Roman Rocks*, 1921. Tempera, 16 x 20"
Collection Zaffagni, Milan

De Chirico: *The Departure of the Knight Errant*, 1923. Tempera, 38 x 50". Collection
Adriano Pallini, Milan

141

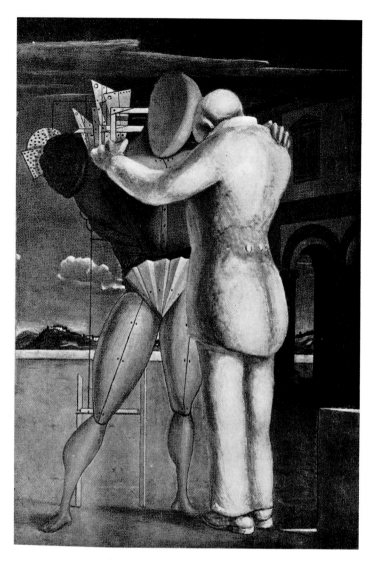

De Chirico: *The Return of the Prodigal*, 1922. Tempera, 34⁷/₈ x 23⁵/₈".
Collection Carlo Frua de Angeli, Milan

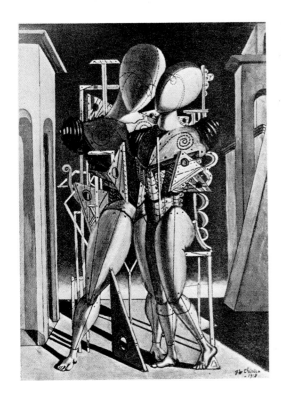

De Chirico: *Hector and Andromache*, 1918(?).
Oil on canvas, 39³/₁₆ x 27¹/₂″. Collection
Mr. and Mrs. Jean de Menil, Houston, Texas

De Chirico: *Hector and Andromache*, 1924. Oil and tempera
on canvas, 39¹/₈ x 28⁵/₈″. Collection R. Toninelli, Milan

De Chirico: *The Grand Metaphysician*, 1917. Oil on canvas,
41¹/₄ x 27¹/₂". Collection Philip L. Goodwin, New York.
(Reproduced in color, page 133)

De Chirico: *The Contemplation of the Infinite*, 1925.
Private collection, Paris

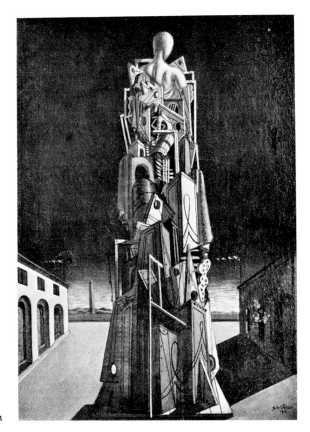

De Chirico: *The Grand Metaphysician*, c.1925(?).
Oil on canvas, 44½ x 32". Collection Adriano Pallini, Milan

De Chirico: *Memory of Italy*, c. 1914. Oil on canvas, 36 × 25¹/₄".
Collection Herbert Rothschild, Kitchawan, New York

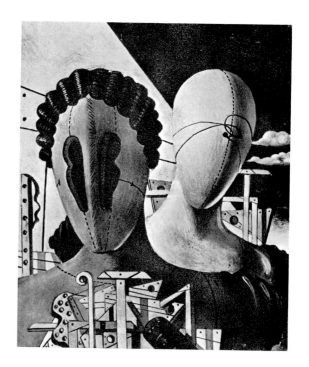

De Chirico: *Two Masks*, 1916(?). Oil on canvas,
22 x 18¹/₂". Collection Emilio Jesi, Milan

De Chirico: *Furniture in the Valley*, c. 1927.
Collection Giovanni Silva, Modena

De Chirico: *The Poet and His Muse*, c. 1925(?).
Oil on canvas, 35¹/₄ x 28¹/₂". The Philadelphia Museum
of Art, Louise and Walter Arensberg Collection

147

De Chirico: *Horses by the Sea*, 1926.
Private collection, Paris

De Chirico: *Perseus Rescuing Andromeda*, c. 1950. Oil on canvas,
36³/₈ x 46¹/₂″. Collection the artist

In 1950 André Breton, surrealism's central figure, published in the *Almanach Surréaliste du Demi Siècle* a retouched reproduction of de Chirico's *The Child's Brain*
(1914) page 193, showing the nude man with his eyes
opened. Breton took typical surrealist delight in the
fact that the change went unnoticed by nearly all the
Almanach's readers.

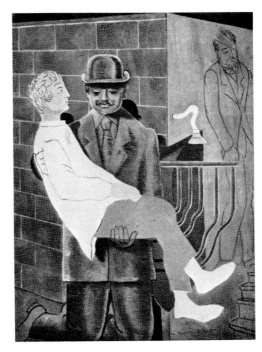

Ernst: *Revolution by Night*, 1923. Oil on canvas,
46 × 35¹/₄". Collection Roland Penrose, London

In 1919 Max Ernst, one of surrealism's most inventive
artists, became deeply impressed by de Chirico's early
paintings. The mustachioed figure in Ernst's *Revolution
by Night* of 1923 refers specifically to the man in de
Chirico's *The Child's Brain*.

Dali: *Nostalgic Echo*, 1935. Oil on canvas, 38 x 38". Collection Mrs. L. M. Maitland, Brentwood, California

As early as 1923 Salvador Dali, then very young, was exposed in Madrid or Barcelona to the art of de Chirico's and Carrà's *scuola metafisica*, as published in *Valori Plastici*. Carrà's influence was of brief duration, but throughout much of his mature career Dali has used de Chirico's infinity of space, punctuated by mysterious shadows and abruptly scaled-down figures, as the setting for his Freudian, pictorial scenarios. De Chirico's example helped decide the young Catalan painter to move to Paris and join the surrealist movement in 1929. The affinity of Dali's *Nostalgic Echo* to de Chirico's early paintings is evident; its girl skipping rope is probably a direct allusion to the child with a hoop in *The Mystery and Melancholy of a Street* (page 73).

Delvaux: *Woman with a Rose*, 1936. Oil on canvas, 52 x 36". Collection Albert Lewin, New York

Paul Delvaux, a year older than his Belgian compatriot, René Magritte, matured comparatively slowly as a painter. Like Magritte he was obviously impressed by de Chirico's conversion of deep, architectural perspective into an evocative, poetic instrument. His relationship to de Chirico is apparent in the *Woman with a Rose* of 1936 and numerous more recent paintings.

Magritte: *The Reveries of a Solitary Promenader*, 1926.
Collage. Collection E. L. T. Mesens, London

Tanguy: *Mama, Papa Is Wounded*, 1927. Oil on canvas,
36¹/₄ x 28 ³/₄″. The Museum of Modern Art, New York

Vast space and heavy, dramatic shadows are recurrent
stylistic devices in de Chirico's paintings of Italian
squares. Their meaning for surrealist artists like Magritte and Yves Tanguy is apparent in the two pictures
here reproduced. Indeed, de Chirico's immense influence
on surrealism is epitomized by an experience recounted
by Tanguy. Riding on a Paris bus one day in the mid-
1920s, Tanguy saw a painting in a gallery window. It
attracted him so forcibly that he jumped off the bus and
ran over to examine it. It was an early de Chirico and
then and there Tanguy decided what direction his own
art would take. He afterwards learned that André Breton
had first come upon de Chirico's pictures in precisely the
same way.

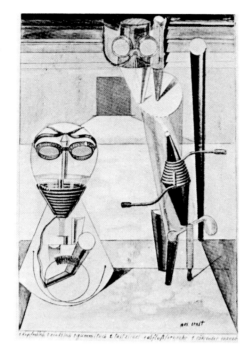

Ernst: *I copper plate I lead plate I rubber towel 2 key rings I drain pipe I roaring man*, 1920. Colored collage. Collection Hans Arp, Meudon, France

The influence of de Chirico on Ernst is apparent in the latter's collage of 1920, notably in the inclusion of a mannequin-like head with glasses and in the deep spatial arrangement which may be compared to that in de Chirico's *The Scholar's Playthings* (page 238)

Magritte: *The Difficult Crossing*, 1926. Oil on canvas, 32³/₈ x 26". Collection Mlle Elisabeth Barman, Brussels

Soon after the First World War a reproduction of de Chirico's *The Song of Love* (color plate, page 77) was seen by the Belgian painter, René Magritte, who soon thereafter also saw *Valori Plastici*'s 1919 monograph on the Italian artist. The impact of de Chirico's early pictures was a determining factor in Magritte's decision to become a surrealist painter. The latter's *The Difficult Crossing* of 1926 recalls de Chirico's metaphysical interiors.

more and more interested in the sensuous qualities of heavy pigment, leaving far behind the bare impasto of his earlier years in Paris. At the same time he now tended to use a much oilier medium than before, a tendency which was to be continued in 1919. The *Metaphysical Interior with Waterfall* seems a typical work of 1918, its technical preoccupations reflected in the few authentic works of the same year which have come to light. But the study of these works is complicated by the fact that the artist or forgers have sometimes dated as 1918 pictures which belong in style neither to the high Ferrarese creative span of 1915–17 nor to de Chirico's neo-classicism of the early 1920s, as though the closing year of the First World War provided a sort of neutral ground, beyond dispute, between admirers of the painter's early and late periods. The number of true 1918 pictures is in any case small. Perhaps during the hectic closing months of the war de Chirico found less time to paint. Perhaps he was then troubled by the conflict between his youthful inspiration, then on the wane, and his rising ambition to become an authoritative and dazzling technical master of his medium.

We know at any rate one or two significant events in his artistic life which took place soon after the war's end. In the winter of 1918–19 he was demobilized and left Ferrara for Rome. And in the latter city in 1919 he had what he has optimistically and luridly described in his autobiography as a "revelation":

It was in the Museum of the Villa Borghese one morning, standing before a Titian, that I received the revelation of what great painting was: in the gallery I beheld tongues of flame; outside, through the vastness of the bright sky, a solemn clangor echoed over the city and trumpets blared announcing a resurrection . . . Until then in museums in Italy, France and Germany, I had looked at pictures and I had seen them as everyone sees them. I had seen them *as images.* Naturally what was revealed to me in the Museum of the Villa Borghese was only a beginning. Later through study, work, observation and meditation I made giant strides and I now understand painting in such a way that when I see the others—those who don't know, who grope in the dark striving in a thousand ways to save face, to deceive themselves and others, who not succeeding are unhappy and being unhappy are bad—then, as I was saying, when I see this sad and discouraging spectacle I am filled with pity for these unfortunates and I would like to offer myself, to hold out my bare chest to these derelicts and cry out to them "Pound! Pound!" and I would like to embrace and kiss them and weep and sob with them and, between sobs, to make them happy, I would swear to them solemnly *that I would paint no more!*[119]

As tangible evidence of de Chirico's new devotion to native traditions in art he completed, during the summer of 1919, a copy of Lorenzo Lotto's *Portrait of a Man in Black* in the galleries of the Villa Borghese. And the following year he copied Michelangelo's *Holy Family* at the Uffizi in Florence. De Chirico's copy of the latter picture still exists (page 138). It is a quite literal copy, though the handling of the Madonna's face and arms foretells de Chirico's personal translation of Mannerist distortions of contour, soon to replace his metaphysical dislocations of reality. In copying the Michelangelo and in listening to the technical advice of a Russian painter-friend, Lochoff, the artist became interested in tempera and presently, between 1920 and 1922, executed in this medium a series of paintings collectively known as the "Roman Villas."

First, however, he had painted in 1919 a number of pictures which differ from his earlier works in approach and technique. The most ambitious of these is *The Return of the Prodigal* (page 138), obviously inspired by Raphael, which typifies "The Return to Craftsmanship" that de Chirico urged on his fellow-artists in an article by that title published in *Valori Plastici* for November-December, 1919. The picture is far oilier and heavier in impasto than anything the painter had done before and, indeed, the "oily" quality of most of his 1919 paintings is what distinguishes them from previous works, as the widow of Mario Broglio, one of de Chirico's most devoted patrons has pointed out in letters to the writer. *The Return of the Prodigal* is a rather heavy-handed pastiche on Renaissance neo-classicism, though the embracing figures of the father and son retain some of the distraught power of the artist's earlier periods.

THE 1919 STILL LIFES

Of greater intrinsic interest and quality, though less revealing as to the psychological upheaval which the artist underwent after his return to civilian life, are a few 1919 still lifes. The most important of these and one of the principal works of de Chirico's entire career is *The Sacred Fish* (opposite), mentioned in passing as an immense influence on Max Ernst and other Central-European Dadaists in their progress toward surrealism. For twenty-odd years the picture belonged to Mario Broglio, whose widow's recollections of it, in a letter of October 10, 1950 to the writer, are therefore well worth recording: "If you examine the medium, it is oily and sombre, like that of the little portrait of which I have sent you a photograph and which is dated 1919. Both paintings evidently were painted in artificial light."[120]

The oiliness and sombreness of *The Sacred Fish* are not the only clues to the fact that it was painted in 1919 and not in 1915 or 1917 as often published. In composition the picture is closely related to another dated work of 1919—the *Hermetic Melancholy* (page 240), which was brought to this country by a partner of Broglio and was subsequently destroyed by fire. Both paintings have a central image—smoked whitefish in one, a plaster head in the other—enclosed by rounded wings, unlike any of the stage-like properties de Chirico had used before. Both seem to have been painted in artificial light, as Mme Broglio points out and, as she goes on to say: "In fact in both pictures the 'metaphysical' element, reduced to *coulisse*, gives way to 'after nature' . . ."[121] The

OPPOSITE: *The Sacred Fish*, 1919. 29⁹/₁₆ x 24¹/₄". The Museum of Modern Art, New York. Acquired through the Lillie P. Bliss Bequest

same rounded wing appears, too, in a richly painted still life of salami (page 239) dated 1919. And the new realism of modeling, suggestive of artists as divergent as Courbet and Manet, prevails in another small still life of 1919 in the Gualino collection at Rome. Obviously de Chirico had now become absorbed in those problems of technical flourish which he had once thought secondary to the quest for philosophical implication and imaginative intensity. It therefore seems curious that his articles eulogizing artists like Böcklin and Klinger should have appeared (in the magazine *Il Convegno*) as late as 1920 rather than much earlier, when the effect of his Germanic training as a painter was more consistently apparent in his works. But perhaps the articles had been written before or during the First World War and held in his notebooks until he could find a publisher. The theory seems plausible when we remember that de Chirico throughout the period between his arrival in Paris (1911) and his departure from Ferrara (1918–19) was interested in writing, as the Eluard and Paulhan manuscripts, here published as Appendices A and B, testify.

Though *The Sacred Fish* was undoubtedly executed in 1919, after de Chirico's enigmatic vision had begun to be qualified by a rising respect for tradition and technical ingenuity in art, it remains one of the most idiosyncratic and memorable of all his works. Its attraction for fantasists like Max Ernst is easy to understand. For here, presented in terms of extreme realism, is a pictorial counter-logic based on subconscious sources of inspiration soon to be explored by the surrealists. The brilliant smoked fish are placed on a platform at the front of a stage and become the protagonists of a strange drama of the inanimate. They are accompanied by unreasonable objects—a toy-like form and a candlestick with a starfish impaled on its wick—the known and the impossible combined to create a believable entity. As noted earlier, *The Sacred Fish* and *The Song of Love* were probably the most influential of de Chirico's still lifes among those artists who became leaders of the surrealist movement (see pages 149–152).

TWO PORTRAITS OF 1919

In Rome after the war de Chirico lived with his mother at the Park Hotel. And it was probably in his rooms at the hotel that he painted, in 1919, the rather remarkable double portrait of himself and his mother (page 137). The foreground image of the mother dominates the picture, as she in person had dominated her two sons in real life. Indeed, persons who knew the de Chirico family during this post-war period have assured the writer that Gemma de Chirico was in every sense a matriarch to whose wishes and demands her sons were subservient, whose advice was law and whom both adored. She appears in her elder son's 1919 portrait as a formidable personality, facing her audience courageously while de Chirico, seen in the background through a window, puts his hand to his lips as though overcome by a mood of meditative indecision. As a psychological document the double portrait is of decided interest. It is painted in the heavy, oily technique characteristic of the still lifes of the same year; the handling of the two pears on the window sill is inescapable evidence of the artist's new interest in solidity of form. The dramatic artificial lighting of both figures indicates that de Chirico, as part of his new absorption in the lessons to be learned from Italy's magnificent past in art, had looked long and hard at paintings by Caravaggio and his followers. And it is interesting to note that the almost marbleized veins on the mother's arm and the pocked skin of the pears were many years later emulated for romantic-decorative purposes by younger artists, notably Eugene Berman.

A small self portrait of the same year (page 137) reminds us forcefully that de Chirico, with seven years of astonishing creative activity to his credit, was still a young man—thirty-one, to be precise. As much as any other artist of our time with the possible exception of Max Beckmann, de Chirico has been fascinated by his own visage and has recorded it at frequent intervals, particularly in recent years. Among these self portraits the two of himself alone and with his mother are outstanding, a fact both pertinent and tragic in that the year 1919 marked the end of his great early career.

1920-24: THE RETURN TO TRADITION

During the early 1920s, before his return to Paris in 1925, de Chirico fluctuated widely in purpose, style and technique as an artist. Dividing his time between Rome and Florence, he studied intently the work of a great number of earlier painters. The single-mindedness and headlong, naïve conviction of his metaphysical period belonged now to the past, and he set out to emulate and rival a bewilderingly disparate group of predecessors, from Dosso Dossi to Courbet, from Signorelli to Rubens, from Raphael to Delacroix. At times he revived themes of his earlier career, as in two paintings of mannequins, respectively dated 1922 and 1924 (pages 142, 143) which reveal a gradual softening of contour in favor of tonal flourish. The two stylistic extremes of his new traditionalism were neo-classicism and the Baroque though, as noted, he railed against the latter historical development in an article, "La Mania del Seicento," published in 1921.[122] (He excepted Poussin and Claude from his general condemnation of seventeenth-century art.) In brief there began in 1920 that desperate attempt on de Chirico's part to become himself a living "old master," with or without credit to his ancestors in the long history of art. The attempt continues to this day and is justified by the painter as a defense of eternal values against the heresies of "modern" art.

Probably no clearer explanation of de Chirico's deliberate reversion to academic standards is to be found than that in a letter written by him from Rome in 1922 to André Breton, a letter herewith reprinted in full because of its exceptional relevance to the collapse of de Chirico as an original, creative artist. It follows:

My very dear friend:

I am very moved by all that you tell me in your good letter. For a long time I worked without hope. Now it's above all necessary that I clarify one point for you: the point which has to do with my painting of today. I know that in France (and even here) there are people who say that I am making a museum art, that I have lost my road, etc. This was fatal and I expected it. But I have an easy conscience and am full of inner joy, for I know that the value of what I am doing will appear sooner or later even to the most blind. The fact that I have made your acquaintance, isn't that already a good sign? The best sign that I could have hoped for?

And now, my dear friend, I am going to speak to you about my present painting. You must have noticed that since some time ago in the arts something has changed; let us not speak of neo-classicism, revival, etc. There are some men, among them probably yourself who, arrived at a limit in their art, have asked themselves, where are we going? They have felt the need of a more solid base; they have renounced nothing. This magnificent romanticism which we have created, my dear friend, these dreams and visions which troubled us and which without control or suspicions we have put down on canvas or paper, all these worlds which we have painted, drawn, written and sung and which are your poesy and that of Apollinaire and a few others, my paintings, those of Picasso, of Derain and a few others—they are always there, my dear friend, and the last word has not been said about them. Posterity will judge them much better than our contemporaries and we can sleep peacefully. But a question, a problem, has tormented me for almost three years: the problem of *métier*. It's for that reason that I began to make copies in the museums, that at Florence and in Rome I spent entire days, summer and winter, before the fourteenth- and fifteenth-century Italians, studying and copying them. I dedicated myself to the reading of ancient treatises on painting and I have seen, yes I have seen at last, that terrible things go on today in painting and that if the painters continue on this route, we are approaching the end. First of all I have discovered (I say "discovered" because I am the only one to say this) that the chronic and mortal malady of painting today is oil pigment, the oil believed to be the base of all good painting. Antonello da Messina, who according to history is supposed to have brought to Italy from Flanders the secret of oil painting, never did that. This misunderstanding springs from the fact that the Flemish, above all the Brothers Van Eyck, used, in going over their tempera works with glazes, emulsions in which linseed or nut oil was contained in small part. But the base of their painting was tempera or distemper with which they sometimes mixed oils and above all resins or still other ingredients like honey, casein, the milk of fig trees, etc. In this fashion without any doubt painted Dürer, Holbein, Raphael, Pietro Perugino, and I believe that even Rubens and Titian never did *oil painting* as we understand it today. When I had comprehended that, I began with the patience of an alchemist to filter my varnishes, to grind my colors, to prepare my canvases and panels, and I saw the enormous difference which was the result. The mystery of color, light, brilliance and all the magic of painting (which, if it may be said without annoying you, my dear friend and great poet) is to my mind the most complicated and magic art there is—all these virtues of painting, I say, expanded prodigiously, as if clarified by a new light. And I thought with melancholy of the impressionists—of Monet, Sisley, Pissarro, and of all these painters who thought to be able to resolve with their technique the problem of light when on their palettes they carried the very source of shadows! And I have painted also. I paint more slowly, it's true, but how much better! I have recently done a self portrait of which I will send you a photo. It is a thing which could figure in the Louvre. I say that not to praise myself but because I think it. Excuse my long peroration about painting and also my poor French, the French of a peninsular barbarian. For today I don't wish to tire you further. I will speak about your poetry, my projects and my arrival in Paris which I hope to be able to arrange this spring.

Thank you again. I embrace you.[123]

De Chirico's enthusiasm for the tempera medium was in good part the result of his technical discussions with Nicola Lochoff. Lochoff was a skilled restorer, whose specialty was the repair and preservation of fresco paintings, and friends describe him as having been a spellbinding lecturer and conversationalist. It is easy to imagine de Chirico, fresh from his labors in copying Michelangelo's *Holy Family* at the Uffizi, deciding to become a creative counterpart to Lochoff as guardian of the great Renaissance past in art. He seems at times to have combined tempera with oil during the early 1920s. But he now abandoned the deliberate oiliness of the 1919 pictures in favor of a new restraint of flat surface.

De Chirico's paintings of the early 1920s, excluding his occasional reversions to his metaphysical period and a few thoroughly Baroque portraits, fall into five main categories as to subject matter. There are, to begin with, the pastiches on Renaissance classicism, typified by *The Departure of the Argonauts* (page 140). Secondly there are the landscapes with statuary (pages 139–140) inspired by the environs of Rome, which move in the direction of Courbet, whose rich impasto would seem at variance with de Chirico's new interest in fresco-like surfaces. The third iconographical category may be described as a kind of romantic classicism, with the villas of the Roman country-side providing the background to activity belonging to the troubadour tradition. *Roman Villa with Knights* and *The Departure of the Knight Errant* (page 141), owing much to Dosso Dossi whose works de Chirico would have seen in abundance at Ferrara, are cases in point. Perhaps the artist by now had become interested in proto-romantics like Salvatore Rosa and in high romantics like Delacroix. At any rate, the pictures in this category follow the Arcadian trend of painters as widely separated in time as Dossi, Poussin and the nineteenth-century romantics. And in the fourth category under discussion—still lifes with ruins and incongruous juxtapositions of inanimate objects—the artist's full romantic nostalgia for times past and departed glories is felt.

There is, however, a fifth group of pictures in tempera, painted by de Chirico during the early 1920s, which deserves mention and qualified praise. These are pictures in which the artist's proto-surrealist fantasy of imagination flares up in certain details. They are paintings once more of Roman villas, but their neo-classicism is disturbed by the curiously phantomic figures which inhabit their terraces or peer out of windows (page 139). Among their virtues, in the historical sense, is that they pave the way for the revival of the *scuola metafisica* which Alberto Savinio and others undertook during the 1930s. They are not, however, to be compared in either quality or prophetic importance to de Chirico's works of 1910–19.

It is a paradox of de Chirico's career that he first attained truly international fame during the early 1920s, when his relationship with those chiefly responsible for this fame–the Dadaists, soon to become surrealism's leaders–was slowly deteriorating. His 1919 exhibition in Berlin, organized by *Valori Plastici*, brought his early art to the attention of the Central European Dadaists. That same year *Valori Plastici* published the first monograph on his work, entitled *12 Opere di Giorgio de Chirico*, with tributes by Soffici, Apollinaire, Vauxcelles, Raynal, J. E. Blanche, Roger Marx, Papini, Carrà and Etienne Charles. The little book reproduces some of de Chirico's principal paintings and drawings of 1917–19 and reached an influential if small group of artists and critics in France, Germany, Belgium and Italy. Reviewing the book, André Breton wrote: "I believe that a veritable modern mythology is in the process of formation. To Giorgio de Chirico belongs the function of fixing it imperishably in memory."[124]

From 1920 to 1925 de Chirico was in correspondence not only with Breton, but with Paul Eluard, who was from 1924 to the outbreak of World War II Breton's principal ally in the surrealist movement. Both Breton and Eluard apparently bought in Paris paintings and drawings which de Chirico had left behind in his studio at no. 9 rue Campagne-Première when he departed for Italy in 1915, the sale having been arranged perhaps by the Italian poet, Ungaretti, then a friend both of de Chirico and the *avant-garde* French writers. And the Biennale of 1923 in Rome was visited by Eluard, who bought additional pictures by de Chirico, and the next year commissioned his copy of *The Disquieting Muses*.

In 1925 de Chirico again exhibited a group of pictures at the Roman Biennale. But whereas two years before he had had a great *succès d'estime* and sold several works to the Breton-Eluard circle, this time, he reports, "there was the silence of a tomb."[125] The chief reason for this silence unquestionably was that the surrealist poets and artists had begun to suspect that de Chirico's metaphysical inspiration was spent, that his conversion to academic painting was final. The twelve issues of *La révolution sur-réaliste*, published between December 1, 1924 and December 15, 1929, reproduced many of de Chirico's early works and included some of his poems of 1911–13. But in the issue of July 15, 1925, Max Morise, reviewing an exhibition of the artist's work at the Galerie de l'Effort Moderne in Paris, expressed in guarded terms the surrealists' belief that de Chirico had become too immersed in classicism and in technical problems. The following March, two paintings by the Italian were reproduced: *The Sarcophagus*, one of his tempera pictures of c.1921 (the most recent de Chirico thus far illustrated by the magazine); and a Raphaelesque figure piece entitled *Orestes and Electra* of 1922–23. The latter picture's reproduction had been scribbled over with black lines by the editors to show their contempt for its derivative neo-classicism.

The quarrel between de Chirico and the surrealists became more and more intense, particularly after the artist's return to Paris in 1925. It reached a climax in 1928, when Breton's *Le surréalisme et la peinture* was published. The book reproduced a number of de Chirico's paintings of 1913–17 (some are erroneously dated) and remains a central source of information about his early work. But Breton's text about the artist is scathing in its denunciation of the latter's art and attitude since his departure from Ferrara after the First World War. For example, it attacks violently the Paris exhibition of de Chirico's paintings held at Paul Guillaume's Gallery in June, 1926, though chiefly because the catalogue of the show contained a preface by the late Dr. Albert C. Barnes (the show itself included mostly early pictures). In 1928 the leading surrealists also published a broadsheet attacking an exhibition of de Chirico's recent pictures at Brussels. From this date on the breach between the painter and the surrealists was never healed; indeed their dispute became thoroughly vituperative and continued so even after the decline of surrealism as a cohesive movement.

The fact remains that until late 1925 or early 1926 the surrealists hoped that de Chirico might regain his creative vitality, and Breton's statement, "We have spent five years now despairing of de Chirico,"[126] published in *La révolution surréaliste* for June 15, 1926, is an exaggeration. Recognizing that de Chirico had been the most important twentieth-century precursor of surrealist art (in every direction except that proposed by the abstract automatism of Duchamp, Arp, Miro and others), Breton and his associates tried by pressure and cajolement to make the Italian artist abandon his technical preoccupations and his revival of classicism. If they had lost faith in him entirely as early as 1920 or 1921, as suggested by Breton's statement, it seems unlikely that Breton and Eluard would have continued to correspond with him until his return to Paris in 1925.

For a time the surrealists' effort to help de Chirico regain his early impetus seemed partially successful. At intervals between 1924 and 1928 (and occasionally later), the painter revived certain subjects of his early period, as he had done in Rome and Florence after the First World War. In 1925, for example, he completed a number of neo-metaphysical works, chiefly mannequin figures and fantastic still lifes; the best of them are reproduced in Léonce Rosenberg's magazine, *Bulletin de l'effort moderne*, for October, 1925, and February, 1926. But the hallucinatory intensity of his early art was spent, as becomes apparent if we compare the reproductions of his paintings of 1925–28 in Waldemar George's monograph, *Chirico*, with the plates illustrating his proto-surrealist art in Breton's *Le surréalisme et la peinture*. Both books were published in 1928, and in a vivid way they summarize de Chirico's rise and decline. Yet it remains to be said that sometimes the artist's extraordinary imaginative gifts flared up in literary form. In 1927 he published in *Bulletin de l'effort moderne* a remarkable description of the animistic quality of furniture seen piled up on the street, ready for the moving van.[127] One senses here a return to the oneiric inspiration of his youth (page 147). But his paintings on the theme are only slightly more convincing than other works of 1927. Similarly, his genius revives in his novel, *Hebdomeros*, published in 1929 and greatly admired even by his now-enemies, the surrealists. As a painter, however, de Chirico after his return to Paris in 1925 was clearly more at ease as a classicist and an exponent of technical virtuosity than as a metaphysician. No amount of prodding by the surrealists or others could revive his youthful, inventive power.

1925-28: PAINTINGS OF CLASSICAL MYTHOLOGY

There were presumably three principal factors underlying de Chirico's return to classicism. The first of these was his absorption in the art of the past, stimulated by his postwar studies in the great museums of Rome and Florence and by his discussions with Nicola Lochoff. The second may well have been his regard for Picasso who, beginning in 1917, had alternately painted classical-realistic pictures and abstract works. Picasso's neo-classic paintings and drawings undoubtedly were known to de Chirico, and it is a significant if inconclusive fact that many of them were partly inspired by Picasso's trip to Rome in 1917 with Diaghilev's Russian Ballet. De Chirico must have taken courage—and learned much—from his Spanish colleague's example.

A third factor, accounting in good part for de Chirico's 1925–28 paintings of ancient ruins, gladiators and wild horses (page 148), was his enthusiasm for Sir James George Frazers's travel account of classical Greece, published in French in 1923 as *Sur les Traces de Pausanias*. The late Alberto Savinio once assured the writer that the painter had read the book with rapt attention, and indeed many of the latter's neoclassic pictures of the later 1920s might serve as illustrations of the Grecian scenes described by Frazer. But as paintings they are tiresomely sweet, even chic, and with them it seems fair to take leave of de Chirico as a vital force in modern art.

In 1919 de Chirico's article for *Valori Plastici*, entitled "Il ritorno al mestiere," had concluded with the statement: *"Pictor classicus sum."*[128] Since the recent war he has often inscribed his paintings "G. de Chirico, *Pictor optimus.*" His work of the past twenty-five years has brought him not respect and fame, but notoriety. Borrowing from an incredible roster of past artists, reverting above all to the Baroque tradition (page 148) which he had once held in contempt, devoting much of his energy to violent attacks on the twentieth-century visual revolution of which he was once an irreplaceable leader, de Chirico has tried with every means at his power to obliterate his own brilliant youth. Fortunately for the history of art he has failed. His early paintings survive and gain steadily in qualitative and historical importance.

Plates

The Enigma of an Autumn Afternoon, 1910. About 14×18″. Private collection, Italy

The Enigma of the Oracle, 1910. About 14 x 18″. Private collection, Italy

165

Self Portrait (What shall I love if not the enigma?), 1911.
28¹/₂ x 21⁵/₈″. Collection Mrs. Stanley Resor, Greenwich, Connecticut

Self Portrait, 1912 (?). 32¹/₂ x 27″. Collection
Carl Van Vechten, New York

166

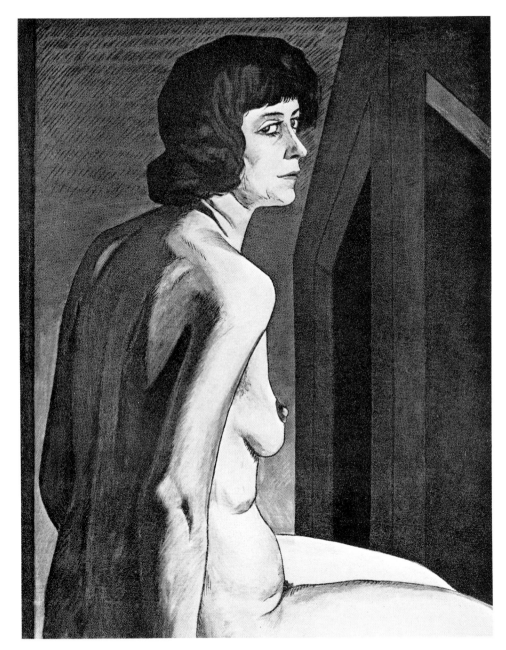

Nude (Etude), 1911–12. 28 x 21¹/₂″. The Pierre Matisse Gallery, New York

The Enigma of the Hour, 1912. 21⅝ x 27⅞". The Gianni Mattioli Foundation, Milan. Feroldi Collection. See photograph of courtyard adjoining the Brancacci Chapel, Church of the Carmine, Florence, page 58

Melancholy, 1912(?) 31 x 25". Collection Peter Watson, London

The Rose Tower, 1913. 29$^{1}/_{2}$ × 39$^{1}/_{2}$″. Collection Miss Peggy Guggenheim, Venice

The Delights of the Poet, 1913. 27³/₈ × 34". The Museum of Modern Art, New York. Acquired through the Lillie P. Bliss Bequest

The Tower, 1911–12. 45³/₈ x 17⁷/₈".
Collection Bernard Poissonnier, Paris

The Great Tower, 1913. 46¹/₄ × 19³/₄".
Collection Bernard Poissonnier, Paris

The Melancholy of a Beautiful Day, 1913. 35 x 41⁷/₈". Collection Benedict Goldschmidt, Brussels

The Lassitude of the Infinite, 1913 (?). 17¹/₄ × 44″. Collection Mrs. John Stephan, New York

The Soothsayer's Recompense, 1913. 52³/₄ × 70¹/₂″. The Philadelphia Museum of Art, Louise and Walter Arensberg Collection

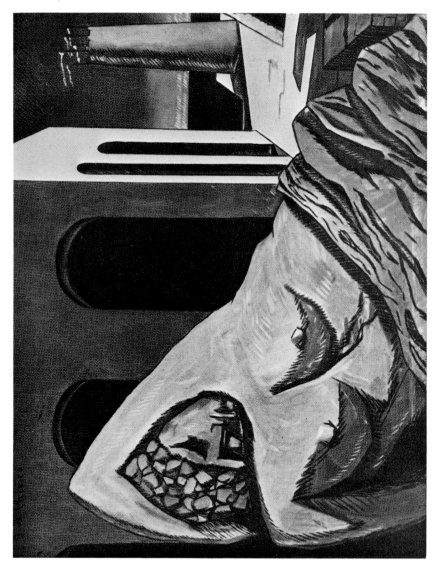

177

Ariadne, 1913. 53 × 70³/₄″. Collection Jean Paulhan, Paris.

Ariadne's Afternoon, 1913. Collection Yvon Delbos, Paris

The Joys and Enigmas of a Strange Hour, 1913. 33 x 51". Collection Wright S. Ludington, Santa Barbara, California

The Anxious Journey, 1913. 29¹/₂ x 42". The Museum of Modern Art, New York. Acquired through the Lillie P. Bliss Bequest

The Chimney, 1913.
Private collection, Paris

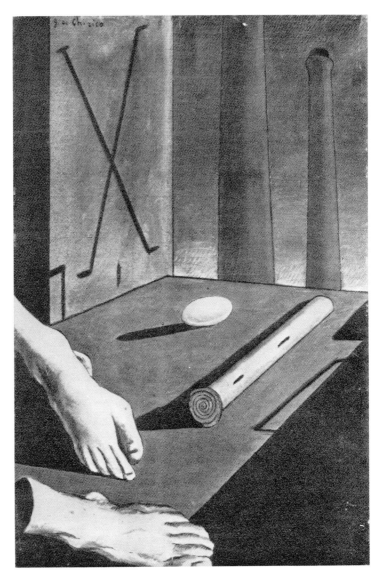

Self Portrait, 1913. 32 x 21¹/₄″. Collection Richard S. Zeisler, New York

The Uncertainty of the Poet, 1913. 41¹/₂ × 37". Collection Roland Penrose, London

The Square, 1913. 22³/₈ × 18⁷/₈".
Collection Bernard Poissonnier, Paris

The Philosopher's Promenade, 1914. 53 × 25¹/₂″. Collection the
Vicomte Charles de Noailles, Paris

The Transformed Dream, 1913. 25 × 62″. The City Art Museum, St. Louis

The Philosopher's Conquest, 1914. 49¹/₂ × 39¹/₂". The Art Institute of Chicago. Purchased for the Joseph Winterbotham Collection

188

OPPOSITE: *The Enigma of a Day*, 1914. 72³/₄ × 55¹/₂". Private collection, New Canaan, Connecticut

The Departure of the Poet, 1914. 34 × 16".
Collection Mrs. L. M. Maitland, Brentwood, California

190

Gare Montparnasse (The Melancholy of Departure), 1914. 55 × 72". Private collection, New Canaan, Connecticut

The Surprise, 1914. 40 × 29″. Collection Mrs. Yves Tanguy, Woodbury, Connecticut

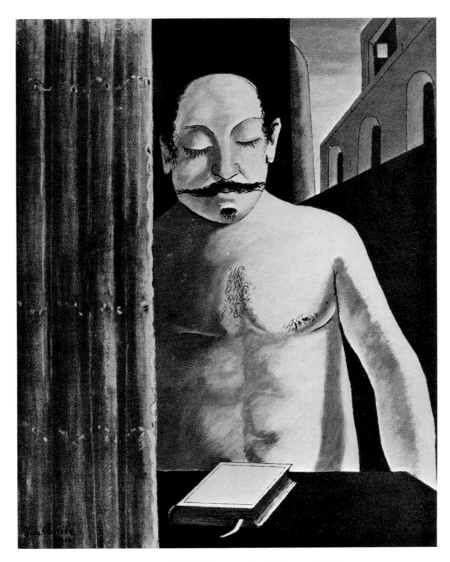

The Child's Brain, 1914. 32 × 25¹/₂″. Collection André Breton, Paris

The Anguish of Departure, 1914. 33½ × 27½″. The Albright Art Gallery, Buffalo, Room of Contemporary Art

The Serenity of the Scholar, 1914. Height 52"; width at bottom 28⅝"
at top 21⅜". Collection Gordon Onslow-Ford, Mill Valley, California

The Destiny of a Poet, 1914. 34^1/$_2$ x 28". Collection Pierre Matisse, New York

Still Life: Turin, Spring, 1914. 48³/₈ × 39¹/₄″. Collection the Vicomte Charles de Noailles, Paris

The Enigma of Fatality, 1914. 54³/₈ × 37¹/₂″.
Collection Bernard Poissonnier, Paris

The Fête Day, 1914. 31³/₄ x 25¹/₂". The Carstairs Gallery, New York

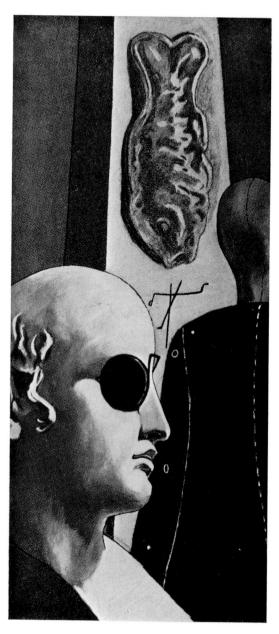

The Dream of the Poet, 1914. 35 x 15½".
Collection Miss Peggy Guggenheim, Venice

200

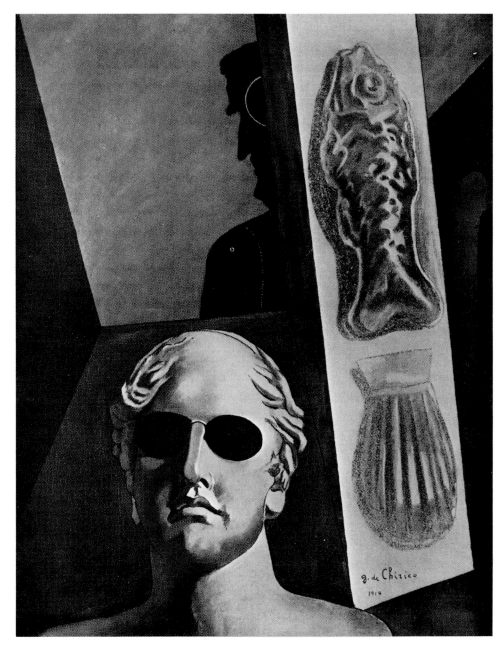

Portrait of Guillaume Apollinaire, 1914. 34 × 27¹/₈". Collection Mme Guillaume Apollinaire, Paris

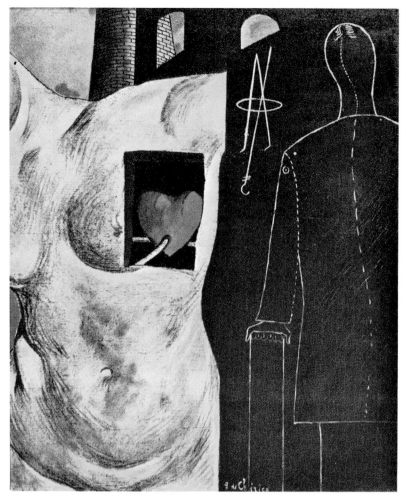

I'll be there ... The Glass Dog, 1914. 27 x 22½". Collection Mr. and Mrs. Bernard Reis, New York.

The Playthings of the Prince, 1914–15. 21³/₄ x 10¹/₈". Collection Mrs. Pierre Matisse, New York

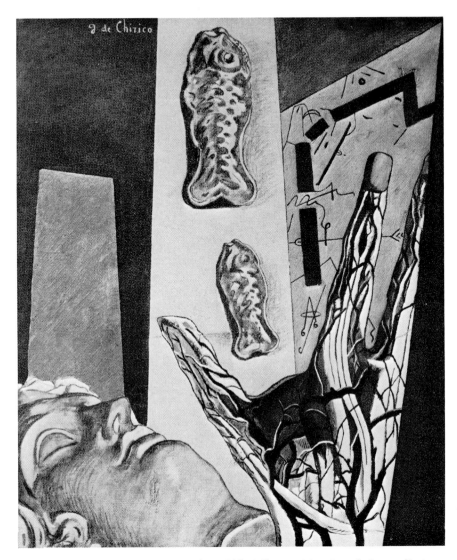

The Span of Black Ladders, 1914. 24¹/₄ × 18⁵/₈". Collection Mme Eyre de Lanux, Paris

The Torment of the Poet, 1914. 20³/₄ × 16¹/₈″. Collection Mrs. Yves Tanguy, Woodbury, Connecticut

The Endless Voyage, 1914. 34½ × 15¼″.
Collection Mrs. Marcel Duchamp, New York

The General's Illness, 1914–15. 23³/₄×17¹/₂″. The Wadsworth Atheneum, Hartford, Connecticut

The Sailors' Barracks, 1914. 32 x 25½". The Norton Gallery of Art, West Palm Beach, Florida

The Inconsistencies of the Thinker, 1915. 18¼ x 15".
The San Francisco Museum of Art

The Prophecy of the Savant, 1915. 18 x 15".
Collection Mr. and Mrs. Burton Cumming,
Westport, Connecticut

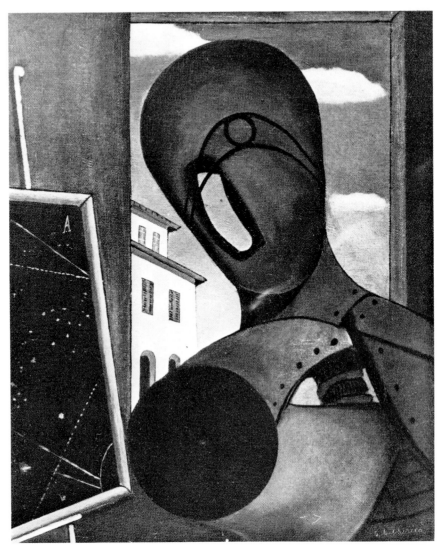

The Astronomer (L'Inquiétude de la mie), 1915. 16¹/₈ × 13″. Collection Mr. and Mrs. Burton Cumming, Westport, Connecticut

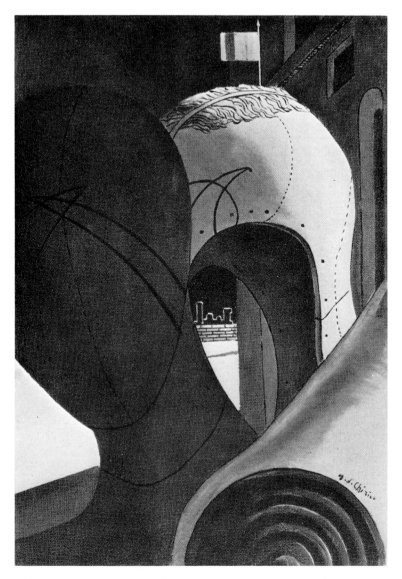

The Fatal Light, 1915. 21¹/₂ x 15″. Collection Miss Peggy Guggenheim, Venice

The Two Sisters, 1915. 26×17″. Collection Roland Penrose, London

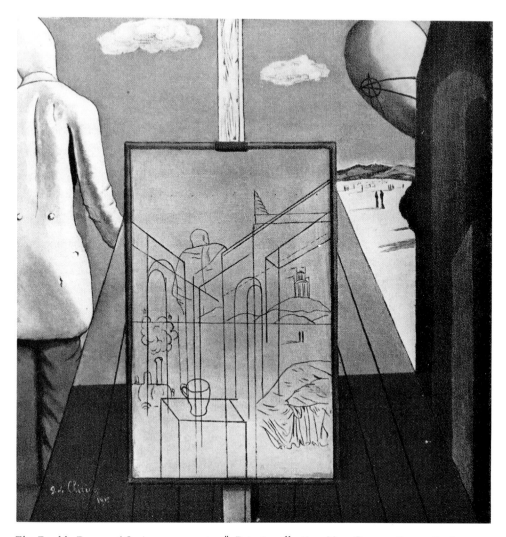

The Double Dream of Spring, 1915. 22 x 21". Private collection, New Canaan, Connecticut

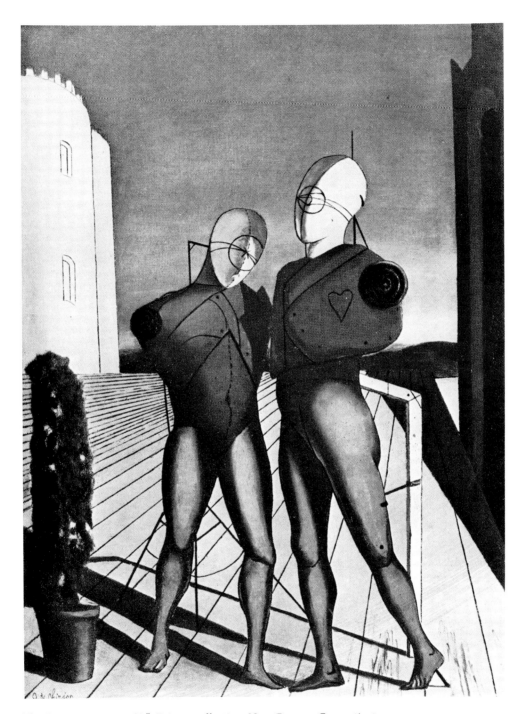

The Duo, 1915. 31 x 22³/₄″. Private collection, New Canaan, Connecticut

The Joy of Return, 1915. 33¹/₂ × 27″. Collection Mrs. L. M. Maitland, Brentwood, California

The Purity of a Dream, 1915. 25⅝ x 19⅞". Collection Bernard Poissonnier, Paris

Portrait of Carlo Cirelli, 1915. 30⁵/₈ x 25¹/₂". Collection Adriano Pallini, Milan

The War, 1916. 13¹/₂ x 10¹/₂".
Collection Gordon Onslow-Ford, Mill Valley, California

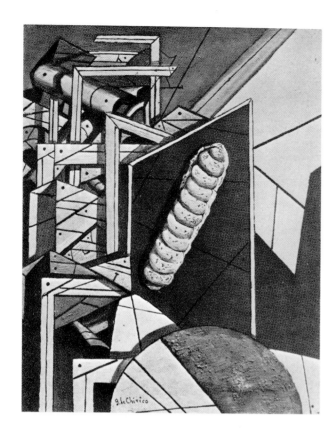

The Homesickness of an Engineer, 1916. 12¹/₂ × 9¹/₂**".**
Collection Mrs. Stanley Resor, Greenwich, Connecticut

The Language of a Child, 1916 (?). 16¹/₄ × 11".
Collection Pierre Matisse, New York

Death of a Spirit, 1916. 14¹/₂ × 13″. Collection E. L. T. Mesens, London

Politics, 1916. 12⁷/₈ × 10¹/₄″. Collection Gordon Onslow-Ford, Mill Valley, California

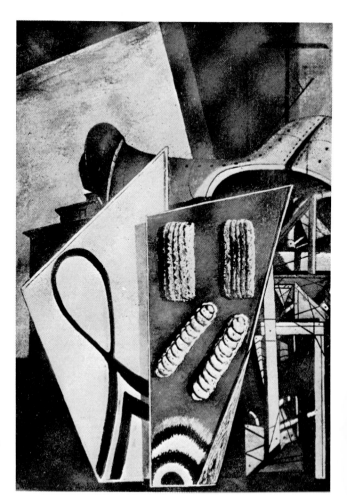

Metaphysical Still Life, 1916. Private collection, Paris (?)

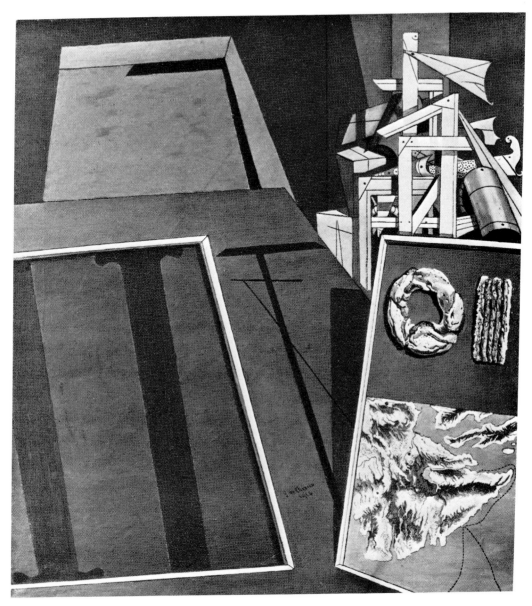

Evangelical Still Life, 1916. 31¹/₂ x 28". Collection Sidney Janis, New York

The Melancholy of Departure, 1916. 20$^1/_2$ x 14$^1/_4$". Collection Roland Penrose, London

The Faithful Servitor, 1916. 15¹/₈ × 13⁵/₈″. Private collection, New Canaan, Connecticut

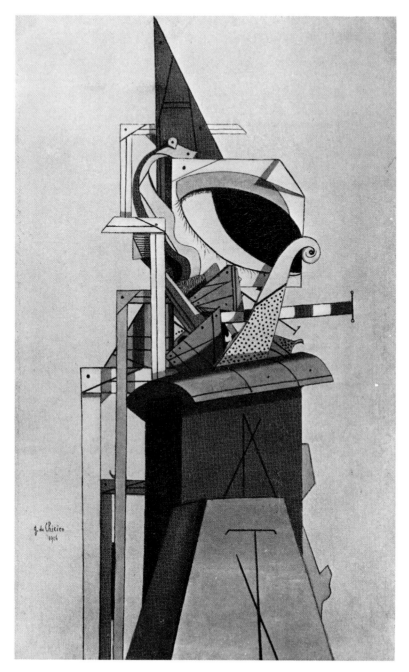

The Jewish Angel, 1916. 26¹/₂ × 17¹/₄″. Collection Roland Penrose, London

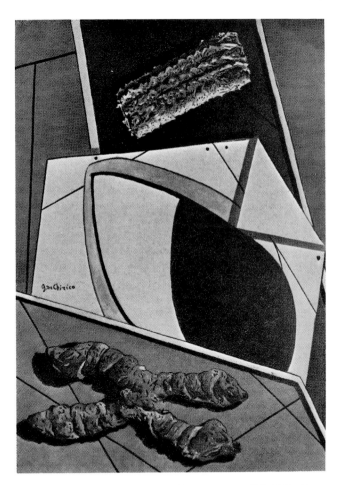

The Greetings of a Distant Friend, 1916. 18 x 13¹/₂″. Collection
Eric Estorick, London

The Regret, 1916. 23¹/₄×13″. Collection Munson-Williams-Proctor
Institute, Utica, New York

226

The Revolt of the Sage, 1916. 26¹/₂ x 23¹/₄″. Collection Sidney Janis, New York

Metaphysical Interior, I, 1916. 12³/₈ x 9⁷/₈. Collection Roland Penrose, London

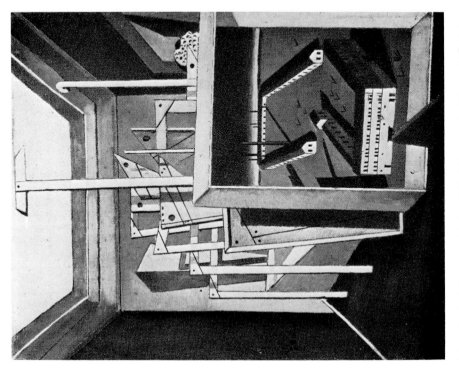

Metaphysical Interior with Small Building, 1916. 18¹/₈ x 14¹/₈″. Collection Carlo Frua de Angeli, Milan

228

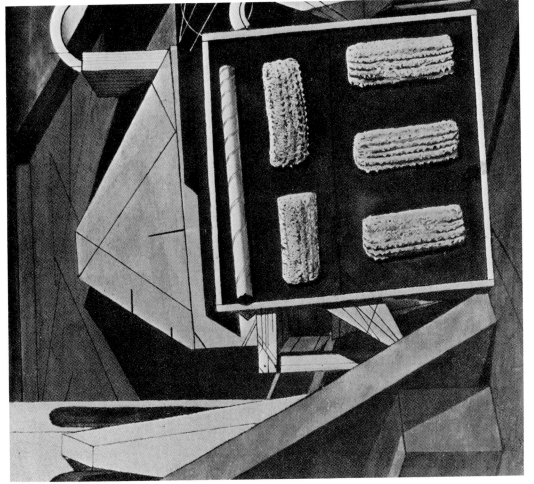

The Gentle Afternoon, 1916. 25³/₈ x 23¹/₄". Collection Miss Peggy Guggenheim, Venice

Metaphysical Interior with Large Building, 1916, 37³/₄ × 28¹⁵/₁₆". Collection Carlo Frua de Angeli, Milan

The Amusements of a Young Girl, 1916. 18 x 15½". Private collection, New Canaan, Connecticut

Hector and Andromache, 1916 (?). Private collection, Germany

Hector and Andromache, 1917. 35½ x 23⅝″. The Gianni Mattioli Foundation, Milan. Feroldi Collection

Troubadour, 1917. 34³/₄ × 20³/₈″. Collection Carlo Frua de Angeli, Milan

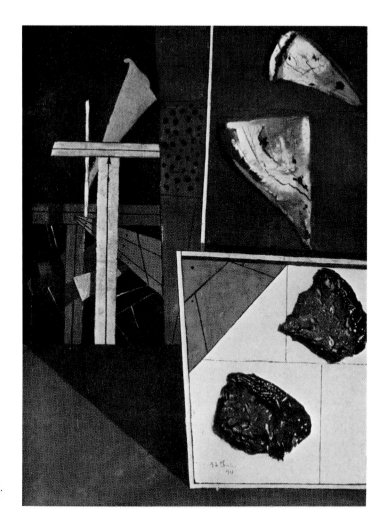

Metaphysical Interior, 1917. 17 × 12″.
Collection Sidney Janis, New York

Metaphysical Interior with Biscuit and Cigarette Holder, 1917.
21⁵/₈ x 13³/₄". Collection Carlo Frua de Angeli, Milan

Metaphysical Interior. Collection Roland Penrose, London

236

Evangelical Still Life, 1917. 35³/₈ x 23¹/₂". Collection Carlo Frua de Angeli, Milan

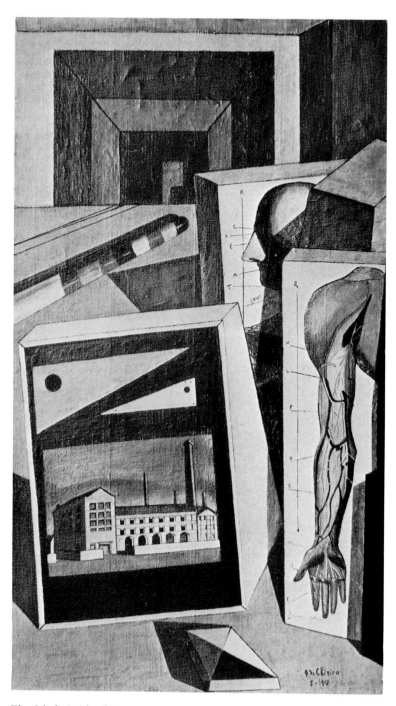

The Scholar's Playthings, 1917. $35^{1}/_{4} \times 20^{1}/_{4}''$. The Pierre Matisse Gallery, New York

238

Metaphysical Interior with Waterfall, 1918. 24¹/₂ × 18¹/₈".
Collection Carlo Frua de Angeli, Milan

Still Life with Salami, 1919. 11³/₄ × 15³/₄".
Collection Giulio Laudisa, Rome

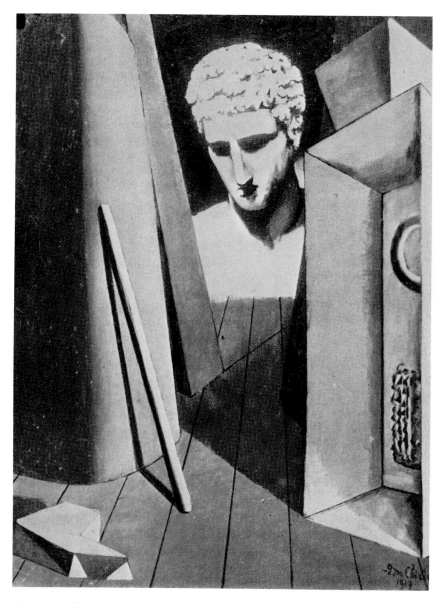

Hermetic Melancholy, 1919. Formerly collection Mario Girardon, Rome. (Destroyed by fire in America)

Notes to the Text

1 Giorgio de Chirico, *Memorie della Mia Vita*, Rome, Astrolabio, 1945, p. 9
2 *Ibid.*, p. 11
3 Giorgio de Chirico, "Le Fils de l'Ingénieur," in Waldemar George, *Chirico avec des fragments littéraires de l'artiste*, Paris, Chroniques du Jour, 1928
4 *La révolution surréaliste*, no. 1, Paris, December, 1924, p. 3
5 *Memorie*, p. 11–12
6 *Ibid.*, p. 66
7 *Ibid.*, p. 36
8 *Ibid.*, p. 53
9 *Ibid.*, p. 83
10 *Ibid.*, p. 84
11 *Memorie*, p. 84
12 Giorgio de Chirico, "Arnoldo Boecklin," *Il Convegno*, No. 4, Milan, 1920, p. 50
13 *Ibid.*, p. 52
14 *Ibid.*, pp. 49, 50, 52
15 Friedrich Nietzsche, *Human, All-Too-Human, Part Two*, pp. 91–92, from *The Complete Works of Friedrich Nietzsche*, edited by Dr. Oscar Levy, New York, The Macmillan Company, 1911
16 Friedrich Nietzsche, *The Birth of Tragedy*, pp. 28–29, from *The Complete Works of Friedrich Nietzsche*, edited by Dr. Oscar Levy, London, T. N. Foulis, 1909
17 *Ibid.*, p. 23
18 *Memorie*, p. 81
19 *Ibid.*, p. 81
20 Friedrich Nietzsche, *Ecce Homo*, p. 120
21 Friedrich Nietzsche, *The Birth of Tragedy*, p. 23
22 Giorgio de Chirico, "Meditations of a Painter," (unpublished article), Paulhan manuscript, Appendix B
23 Giorgio de Chirico, "Arnoldo Boecklin," *Il Convegno*, Milan, May, 1920, p. 47
24 Giorgio de Chirico, "Max Klinger," *Il Convegno*, Milan, Nov., 1920, p. 36
25 *Ibid.*, p. 36
26 *Ibid.*, pp. 37–38
27 *Ibid.*, p. 40
28 Dr. Carlo L. Ragghianti, "Il primo De Chirico," *La Critica d'Arte*, Florence, Nov., 1949
29 Emil Kaufman, in a letter (1950) to the writer
30 *Memorie*, p. 89
31 *Ibid.*, p. 89
32 *Ibid.*, p. 91
33 *Ibid.*, p. 96
34 *Ibid.*, p. 96
35 *Ibid.*, p. 98
36 *Ibid.*, p. 91
37 Giorgio de Chirico, *Courbet*, Rome, Editions de "Valori Plastici," 1925, pp. 8–9
38 *Memorie*, p. 98
39 Giorgio de Chirico, "Le Fils de l'Ingénieur," in Waldemar George, *Chirico avec des fragments littéraires de l'artiste*, Paris, Chroniques du Jour, 1928, p. xxviii
40 *Ibid.*, p. xxix
41 Giorgio de Chirico, "Meditations of a Painter" (unpublished article), Paulhan manuscript, Appendix B
42 *Memorie*, p. 92
43 *Memorie*, p. 92
44 Giorgio de Chirico, "Sull'arte metafisica," *Valori Plastici*, nos. 4–5, Rome, 1919, p. 17
45 James Thrall Soby and Alfred H. Barr, Jr., *Twentieth-Century Italian Art*, The Museum of Modern Art, 1949
46 Pierre Courthion, "L'Art de Giorgio de Chirico," *Sélection*, no. 8, Antwerp, 1929, p. 9
47 Giorgio de Chirico, "La Mania del Seicento," *Valori Plastici*, vol. III, no. 3, Rome, 1921, p. 61
48 Giorgio de Chirico, "Il senso architettonico nella pittura antica," *Valori Plastici*, vol. II, nos. 5–6, Rome, May-June, 1920, p. 60
49 *Memorie*, p. 97
50 *Ibid.*, p. 96
51 Giorgio de Chirico, "Il senso architettonico nella pittura antica," *Valori Plastici*, vol. II, nos. 5–6, Rome, May-June, 1920, p. 59
52 Giorgio de Chirico, "Sull'arte metafisica," p. 17
53 *Ibid.*, p. 17
54 Giorgio de Chirico, "Classicismo Pittorico," *La Ronda*, vol. II, no. 7, Rome, July, 1920, pp. 506–507
55 Giorgio de Chirico, *Courbet*, Rome, Editions de "Valori Plastici," 1925, pp. 8–9
56 Giorgio de Chirico, "Impressionismo," *Valori Plastici*, vol. I, nos. 6–10, Rome, June-Oct., 1919, p. 26

57 Giorgio de Chirico, in Roger Vitrac, *Georges de Chirico*, Paris ("Les Peintres Français Nouveaux," no. 29), 1927, p. 12. The quotation originally came from the Eluard manuscript, Appendix A

58 Giorgio de Chirico, in André Breton, *Le surréalisme et la peinture*, Paris, 1928, p. 38

59 Giorgio de Chirico, Eluard manuscript, Appendix A. The statement was printed in Max Morise's "A propos de l'exposition Chirico," *La révolution surréaliste*, vol. I, no. 4, Paris, July 15, 1925, p. 31; also in Vitrac's monograph (1927), p. 13

60 Philippe Soupault, *Guillaume Apollinaire, ou reflets de l'incendie*, Marseille, Les Cahiers du Sud, 1927, pp. 33—34

61 Mme Guillaume Apollinaire's letter to the present writer is dated June 2, 1950

62 Guillaume Apollinaire, "Salon d'Automne," *Les Soirées de Paris*, no. 18, Paris, Nov. 15, 1913, p. 9

63 Guillaume Apollinaire, "Le 30e Salon des Indépendants," *Les Soirées de Paris*, no. 22, Paris, Mar. 15, 1914, p. 186

64 Guillaume Apollinaire, *L'Esprit Nouveau et les Poètes*, Paris, Jacques Haumont, 1946, p. 17 (original edition, 1918)

65 Roger Shattuck, *Selected Writings of Guillaume Apollinaire*, New York, New Directions, 1949, p. 181

66 André Billy, *Apollinaire Vivant*, Paris Editions de La Sirène, 1923, p. 42

67 Angelo Bardi, "La Vie de Giorgio de Chirico," *Sélection*, no. 8, Antwerp, 1929, p. 20

68 Ardengo Soffici, "Soffici a Milano," *Lacerba*, vol. II, no. 13, Florence, July 1, 1914, p. 207

69 *Memorie*, p. 101

70 Giorgio de Chirico, "Arnoldo Boecklin," p. 52

71 Giorgio de Chirico, "Noi Metafisici," *Cronache d'Attualità*, Rome, Feb. 15, 1919, p. 6. *Cronache d'Attualità* was the organ of the art gallery of Anton Giulio Bragaglia at which de Chirico's first one-man exhibition in Italy was held very early in 1919. The article, together with many of de Chirico's most important pieces on art, is reprinted in: Giorgio de Chirico and Isabella Far, *Commedia dell'Arte Moderna*, Rome, Traguardi, 1945.

72 Paul Eluard, *Donner à Voir*, Paris

73 Giorgio de Chirico, "Noi Metafisici," p. 5

74 Giorgio de Chirico, "Max Klinger," pp. 38–39

75 Giorgio de Chirico, "Noi Metafisici," p. 5

76 Giorgio de Chirico, "Max Klinger," p. 42

77 Giorgio de Chirico, "Sull'arte metafisica," p. 17

78 *Ibid.*, p. 16

79 *Ibid.*, p. 15

80 Giorgio de Chirico, "Sull'arte metafisica," p. 16

81 *Ibid.*, p. 17

82 *Memorie*, p. 28

83 Robert Melville, "The Visitation—1911–17," *London Bulletin*, London, June, 1940, pp. 7–8

84 "Sur les possibilités irrationnelles de pénétration et d'orientation dans un tableau—Giorgio de Chirico: L'Enigme d'une journée." *Le surréalisme au service de la révolution*, no. 6, Paris, May 15, 1933, pp. 13–16

85 James Thrall Soby, "Italy: Two Movements, Two Paintings," *Contemporary Painters*, The Museum of Modern Art, 1948

86 Giorgio de Chirico, "Mystery and Creation," *London Bulletin*, no. 6, 1938, p. 14. Part of the quotation also is found in the Eluard manuscript, Appendix A.

87 See James Johnson Sweeney, *Plastic Redirections in Twentieth Century Art*, The Renaissance Society of the University of Chicago, 1934, p. 72 n.

88 Robert Melville, "The Visitation—1911–17," p. 8. On page 149 of this book *The Child's Brain* is reproduced with the figure's eyes open, as published by André Breton from a retouched plate.

89 E. L.T. Mesens, "René Magritte," *Peintres Belges Contemporains*, Brussels, Les Editions Lumière, 1945 (?), p. 158

90 Guillaume Apollinaire, "Le 30e Salon des Indépendants," *Les Soirées de Paris*, no. 22, Paris, Mar. 15, 1914, p. 186

91 Giorgio de Chirico, "Zeusi l'esploratore," *Valori Plastici*, vol. I, no. 1, Rome, Nov. 15, 1918, p. 10

92 Hans Erni, "The Lucerne Exhibition," Art Museum, Lucerne, Feb. 24—Apr. 7, 1935

93 Giorgio de Chirico, in Roger Vitrac, *Georges de Chirico*, p. 12, and in the Eluard manuscript, Appendix A

94 Giorgio de Chirico, "Sull'arte metafisica," p. 17

95 Raffaele Carrieri, *Giorgio de Chirico*, Milan, Garzanti, 1942, pp. 4–5

96 Albert(o) Savinio, "Les chants de la mi-mort," *Les Soirées de Paris*, nos. 26–27, Paris, July-August, 1914, p. 414

97 Pierre Courthion, "Giorgio de Chirico," *Cahiers d'Art*, no. 5, Paris, June, 1926, p. 115

98 Giorgio de Chirico, "Mystery and Creation," p. 14, and in Eluard manuscript, Appendix A

99 *Memorie*, p. 105

100 André Breton, *Le surréalisme et la peinture*, Paris, NRF, 1928, p. 36

101 *Memorie*, p. 122

102 *Ibid.*, p. 122

103 Dr. Carlo L. Ragghianti, "Il Primo de Chirico," *La Critica d'Arte*, vol. VIII, no. 4, Florence, Nov. 1, 1949, p. 326

104 Giorgio de Chirico, "Il senso architettonico nella pittura antica," p. 60

105 Giorgio de Chirico, "Rafaello Sanzio," *Il Convegno*, no. 3, Milan, 1920

106 *Ibid.*

107 *Memorie*, pp. 122–23
108 A. M. W. Stirling, *The Richmond Papers* (from the correspondence and manuscripts of George Richmond, R. A., and his son, Sir William Richmond, R. A., K. C. B.), London, Heinemann, 1926, p. 44
109 André Billy, *Apollinaire Vivant*, Paris, Editions de La Sirène, 1923, p. 42
110 Carlo Carrà, *La Mia Vita*, Milan, Rizzoli, 1945, p. 228
111 *Memorie*, p. 129
112 *Ibid.*, p. 127
113 Carlo Carrà, *Pittura Metafisica*, second revised edition, Milan, "Il Balcone," 1945, p. 252
114 *Ibid.*, p. 197
115 *Ibid.*, p. 205
116 *La Mia Vita*, p. 210
117 Giorgio de Chirico, "Max Klinger," p. ?
118 *Twentieth-Century Italian Art*, The Museum of Modern Art, 1949, pp. 20–21
119 *Memorie*, pp. 150–51
120 Signora Mario Broglio, in a letter addressed to the writer, Oct. 10, 1950
121 *Ibid.*
122 Giorgio de Chirico, "La Mania del Seicento"
123 De Chirico's letter to André Breton was published in *Littérature*, edited by Breton and Philippe Soupault, no. 1, Paris, March, 1922 (Nouvelle Série)
124 André Breton
125 *Memorie*, p. 179
126 André Breton, "Le surréalisme et la peinture," *La révolution surréaliste*, no. 7, Paris, June 15, 1926, p. 3
127 G. de Chirico, "Statues, Meubles et Généraux," *Bulletin de l'effort moderne*, Oct., 1927
128 Giorgio de Chirico, "Il ritorno al mestiere," *Valori Plastici*, vol. I, nos. 11–12, Rome, Nov.-Dec., 1919, p. 19

Appendix A: Manuscript from the Collection of the Late Paul Eluard

NOTE: Appendices A and B are translations of manuscripts written by de Chirico during his first Paris period, 1911–1915.

FIRST PART

What impressionism should be:

A building, a garden, a statue, a person—each makes an *impression* upon us. The problem is to reproduce this impression in the most faithful possible fashion. Several painters have been called impressionists who at bottom were not. In my opinion there is no point in using technical means (divisionism, pointillism, etc.) to try to give the illusion of what we call truth. For example, to paint a sunlit landscape trying in every way to give the sensation of light. Why? I too see the light; however well it may be reproduced, I also see it in nature, and a painting that has this for its purpose will never be able to give me the sensation of something new, of something that, previously, *I have not known*. While if a man faithfully reproduces the strange sensations that he feels, this can always give new joys to any sensitive and intelligent person.

Impressionism and sensationalism: Those French impressionist painters whom I would rather call sensationalists follow an excellent path. I believe thay are far ahead of the poets and writers who are their contemporaries. In any case there is much more novelty in what they do than in the whole of modern literature. I am talking of their work in so far as I compare it with the impression that modern painting as a whole makes on me. However I must add that though the road they follow is a good one, it is absolutely opposed to the one I follow, for I believe that one must never forget that a picture must always be the reflection of a profound sensation, and that profound means strange, and strange means uncommon or altogether unknown. Well, what is the impressionist method of procedure: they see something: a landscape, a figure, a still life; then using a certain technique to imitate what they see, they try to give to whoever looks at their painting a sensation which what they have reproduced could not give if it were seen in nature. Thus M. Cézanne, in painting a still life—a napkin with big squares, and some tomatoes or fruits—succeeds in giving us a *sensation* which could not be given by all the still lifes of the museums in which the fruits and vegetables are much truer—in the meaning generally given to truth, of course. It is a fact that this kind of painting is better than what is done generally; nevertheless, there are unfortunately limits to this, and besides, if one is sincere one must admit that in such a conception of art chance often, not to say always, plays a large role in what the painter does.

In my way of thinking and working, the problem is different. Revelation always plays the principal role. A picture reveals itself to us, while the sight of *something* does not reveal a picture; but in this case the picture will not be a faithful copy of *that* which has caused its revelation, but will resemble it vaguely, as the face of someone seen in a dream resembles that person *in reality*. And in all this, technique plays no role; the whole *sensation* will be given by the linear composition of the picture, which in this case always gives the impression of being something unchangeable, where chance has never entered.

A revelation can be born of a sudden, when one least expects it, and also can be stimulated by the sight of something—a building, a street, a garden, a square, etc. In the first instance it belongs to a class of strange sensations which I have observed in only one man: Nietzsche. When Nietzsche talks of how Zarathustra was conceived, and says: "I was surprised by Zarathustra," in this participle—surprised, is contained the whole enigma of sudden revelation.—When [on the other hand] a revelation grows out of the sight of an arrangement of objects, then the work which appears in our thoughts is closely linked with the circumstance that has provoked its birth. One resembles the other, but in a very strange way, like the resemblance there is between two brothers, or rather between the image of someone we know seen in a dream, and that person in reality; it is, and at the same time it is not, that same person; it is as if there had been a slight and mysterious transfiguration of the features. I believe and have faith that, from certain points of view, the sight of someone in a dream is proof of his metaphysical reality—in certain accidental occurences that sometimes happen to us; in the manner and the arrangement that things appear to us and awaken in us unknown sensations of joy and surprise: the sensations of revelation. *Paris*

244

Nietzsche very properly remarks: "With the greatest respect one says of a man 'He is a character.' Yes—if he exhibits a coarse logic, a logic obvious to the eyes of the least discerning. But as soon as it is a question of a more subtle and profound spirit, which is coherent in its own way—a superior way, the observer denies the existence of a character."

The same observation can be made on art, and also on painting. A profound picture will be entirely without the gesticulations, the idealism which attracts the attention of the crowd and makes the name of an artist well-known. All momentary posture, all forced movement will be put aside. Calm, tranquillity, even serenity, but *in* this serenity, as in an eternal lamentation, all *pathos* known until now; all grandeur, all sublimity men have known, their hopes and fears, their joys and their suffering, friendship and love, all will blend their music; but the real value of such a work of art will lie in its new song, for more important than all these will always be the new thing that the artist has brought out of the void, something which, previously, *did not exist.*

There are many more enigmas in the shadow of a man who walks in the sun than in all the religions of the past, present and future.

The Summer Evening: Yesterday, I saw a picture by van Gogh. A landscape: trusses of hay, a mountain in the distance, a warm and sultry summer evening; behind the mountain appears the moon—red and gigantic. Summer evenings, when it is hot, have a poetry of their own—a heart-rending lamentation. In this picture one feels this poetry; one feels it also in the music of M. Rabaud's *Daughter of Roland,* above all in the melody, *Mariez Joyeuse avec des Duvandel.* It is something beautiful, terrible and profound. I have perceived it also in some of Titian's pictures.

To be really immortal a work of art must go completely beyond the limits of the human: good sense and logic will be missing from it.

In this way it will come close to the dream state, and also to the mentality of children.

I remember that often having read Nietzsche's immortal work "Thus Spake Zarathustra," I derived from various passages of this book an impression I had already had as a child when I read an Italian children's book called "The Adventures of Pirouchio." Strange similarity which reveals the profundity of the work. Here there is no naïveté; there is none of the naïve grace of the primitive artist; the work possesses a strangeness similar to the strangeness that the sensation of a child sometimes has, but at the same time that he who created it did so consciously. In the same way I believe that in order to be truly profound a picture must attain this

ground. Böcklin and Poussin reached the utmost limits of painting; one final effort and painting too will have its picture that will carry us *beyond all pictures.*

In the middle ages the study of nature led astray those artists who created *Gothic art.* One can observe the same phenomenon among modern artists: poets, painters and musicians. The truly profound work will be drawn up by the artist from the innermost depths of his being. There is no murmur of brooks, no song of birds, no rustle of leaves. The Gothic and Romantic disappear, and in their stead appear measurements, lines, forms of eternity and infinity. This is the feeling produced by Roman architecture. This is why I believe that Greek and Roman buildings, and all those which later were fashioned upon the same principles, even though somewhat transformed are what is most profound in *art.*

No Music: Music cannot express the essence of sensation. One never knows what music is about, and after all, having heard any piece of music, whether by Beethoven, Wagner, Rossini, or Monsieur Saint-Saëns, every listener has the right to say, and can say, what does this mean? In a profound painting, on the contrary, this is impossible; one must fall silent when one has penetrated it in all its profundity, when one turns the corner of all its walls, and not of its walls alone. Then, light and shade, lines and angles begin to talk, and music too begins to be heard, that hidden music that one does not hear. What I listen to is worthless: there is only what I see with my eyes open—and even better closed. There is no mystery in music; that is precisely why it is the art people enjoy most, for they always discover in it more *sensations.* I felt this last night; yes, I felt it in a profound and silent fashion, in a fashion filled with terror. Should I perhaps call such an experience a truth?

But such truths do not talk, they have no voice; still less do they sing; but sometimes they look at one, and at their glance one is forced to bow one's head and say, *yes, that is true.* What results—a picture, for example, always has a music of its own; that is inevitable, that is the mysterious destiny of all things to have a thousand souls, a thousand aspects.

I felt this yesterday at evening: painting, painting: In my picture: the end of the meal or the music of shattered light, this sensation beyond music is written in letters of fire. Music remains confined, something one takes before the meal or after, but which is not a meal in itself. Here is an enigma which I do not advise imaginative minds to dwell upon too long, for in spite of its afternoon warmth, it is icy. But what joy, great God, what joy you give me when I understand. Is this life, or its opposite, or is it neither one nor the other? Yet it makes me happy, I would not desire it to be otherwise, although who knows, perhaps it is otherwise, and perhaps also . . .

G. C.

When after having left the Munich Academy, I realized that the road I was following was not the one I should follow and I entered upon tortuous paths; some modern artists, especially Max Klinger and Böcklin, captivated me. I thought of those profoundly *felt* compositions, having a particular mood [Stimmung] which one recognized among a thousand others. But once again I understood that this was not what I sought. I read; a passage from Homer enthralled me—Ulysses on Calypsos island; some descriptions, and the picture rose before me, and then I felt I had finally found something. Or while reading Ariosto: Roger, the typical knight-errant rests beneath a tree, he sleeps, his horse crops the grass nearby, all is silent and solitary, one would expect to see a dragon fly by. The scene enchants me, suddenly I conjure up the knight, the horse, the landscape; it is nearly a revelation, but I am still not satisfied. Could not Mantegna, Dürer, Böcklin, [Hans] Thoma or Max Klinger have painted such a picture? Something new is needed.

Then during a trip I made to Rome in October, after having read the works of Friedrich Nietzsche, I became aware that there is a host of strange, unknown, solitary things which can be translated into painting. I meditated a long time. Then I began to have my first revelations. I drew less, I even somewhat forgot how to draw, but every time I did it was under the drive of necessity. Then I understood certain vague sensations which I had previously been unable to explain. The language that the things of this world sometimes speak; the seasons of the year and the hours of the day. The epochs of history too: prehistory, and the revolutions in thought throughout the ages, modern times—all appeared strange and distant. *Subjects* no longer came to my imagination, my compositions had no *sense*, above all no *common sense*. They were calm: but each time I looked at them I experienced exactly what I had experienced at the moment of their conception, which is the most irrefutable proof of their profound worth.

Above all a great sensitivity is needed. One must picture everything in the world as an enigma, not only the great questions one has always asked oneself—why was the world created, why we are born, live and die, for after all, as I have said, perhaps there is no reason in all of this. But rather to understand the enigma of things generally considered insignificant. To perceive the mystery of certain phenomena of feeling, of the character of a people, even to arrive at the point where one can picture the creative geniuses of the past as things, very strange things that we examine from all sides. To live in the world as if in an immense museum of strangeness, full of curious many-colored toys which change their appearance, which, like little children we sometimes break to see how they are made on the inside, and, disappointed, realize they are empty. The invisible tie that joins a people to its creations. Why for instance are the houses in France built in a certain style and not in another. There is no use citing history and the causes of this and of that; this describes, but it explains nothing for the eternal reason that there is nothing to explain, and yet the enigma always remains. The dormer windows on the roofs of the houses in Paris always produce a strange impression in me; I believe there is an unknown force which has driven the architects to make these *dormers*, to *feel* them. I see a link between the dormer window and the red trousers of the French soldier, and the characters of the revolution, and a thousand other things which I cannot explain, and this is true for all peoples, all periods, all countries. I have talked of all these strange things to suggest the degree of intelligence and sensibility at which an artist must arrive in order to conceive what I mean by a picture.

What is needed above all, is to rid art of all that has been its familiar content until now; all subject, all idea, all thought, all symbol must be put aside. If I still accept something of Max Klinger, it is not as a thinker, a symbolist or a scholar; it is because he *invented* something which had not previously existed, something that can be seen in fragments here and there. Only he did not have enough force to *understand* the inner recesses of his heart; that corner which is the most profound, the most mysterious and finally the truest, to look only into this corner, and to see only through this corner.

To have the courage to *give up* all the rest. There is the artist of the future: someone who renounces something every day, whose personality daily becomes purer and more innocent. For even without following in someone else's footsteps, as long as one is subject to the direct influence of something someone else *also knows*, something one might read in a book or come upon in a museum, one is not a creative artist as I understand the term. Above all what is needed is great confidence in oneself. The revelation we have of a work of art, the conception of a picture *must* represent something which has sense in itself, has no subject, which from the point of view of human logic *means nothing at all*. I say that such a revelation (or if you like, conception), must be felt so strongly, must give us such joy or such pain, that we are obliged to paint, impelled by a force greater than the force which impels a starving man to bite like a wild beast into the piece of bread he happens to find.

246

That is what the painting of the future must be. It is impossible that there are many men living who can paint in this way. But perhaps a time will come when one will take into consideration only work painted under the conditions I have just described. I have said that there cannot be many such men. But I believe that there could be more of them than there are at present. For they do exist. I have known some of these men, gifted with a great sensitivity, able to feel unknown things, upon whom people and things do not make the impression *that they generally do*. If such men were better guided, if they could renounce, know what they should renounce and above all divide and separate, and not confuse the sensations peculiar to each of us, which we know someone else could never have with those reflected sensations (whether of a man, a work of art, or a period), which sometimes please us but which never succeed in producing the cold shiver, the profound and solitary joy of revelation: composition conceived for itself, strange and senseless, in which we perceive a whole world that no one knows, a world of which we are perhaps the only inhabitants.

I myself did not suddenly arrive at this conception of painting.

The possession of this important good fortune, there is the enigma of the French spirit. And aside from this, I believe that all these sensations, these voices, these forms having no well defined meaning, have always existed.

One bright winter afternoon I found myself in the courtyard of the palace at Versailles. Everything looked at me with a strange and questioning glance. I saw then that every angle of the palace, every column, every window had a soul that was an enigma. I looked about me at the stone heroes, motionless under the bright sky, under the cold rays of the winter sun shining *without love* like a profound song. A bird sang in a cage hanging at a window. Then I experienced all the mystery that drives men to create certain things. And the creations seemed still more mysterious than the creators. It is futile to explain certain things scientifically, nothing is achieved. The palace was as I had imagined it. I had a presentiment that this was the way it must be, that it could not be different. An invisible link ties things together, and at that moment it seemed to me that I had already seen this palace, or that this palace had once, somewhere, already existed. Why are these round windows an enigma? Why are they—and can only be—French? They have a strange expression. Something altogether superficial like the smile of a child who does not know why he smiles; or something ferocious, like a chest pierced by a sword, or like the wound produced by a sword. And then more than ever I felt that everything was inevitably there, but for no reason and without any meaning.

There is nothing like the enigma of the *Arcade*—invented by the Romans. A street, an arch: The sun looks different when it bathes a Roman wall in light. In all this there is something more mysteriously plaintive than in French architecture.

And less ferocious too. The Roman arcade is a fatality. Its voice speaks in enigmas filled with a strangely Roman poetry; shadows on old walls and a curious music, profoundly blue, having something of an afternoon at the seaside, like these lines of Horace:

> *Ibis Liburnis inter alta navium*
> *Amica propugnacula ...*

SECOND PART: THE FEELING OF PREHISTORY

I write this second part in order that profound minds will forgive me for the first part. And it is through this second part that the said minds will *perhaps* understand what I am driving at.

The problem of what an artist should do becomes more and more disturbing. Nothing is profound enough, nothing pure enough. Everything that has satisfied painters until now **to us** seems child's-play; this is why we look behind barriers in search of *something new*. Is it a dream, or a vision? Artists used to like to dream; their sweet souls fell asleep in the moonlight, to the sound of a flute, on a woman's scented breast.

All this has *vanished*. Yet our minds are haunted by visions; they are anchored to everlasting foundations. In public squares shadows lengthen their mathematical enigmas. Over the walls rise nonsensical towers decked with little multicolored flags; infinitude is everywhere, and everywhere is mystery. One thing remains, immutable as if its roots were frozen in the entrails of eternity: our will as artist-creators.

Will we regret the *other* things? Never. Our joy is only greater. Let us work!

G. C.
Paris, June 15, 1913

Inside a ruined temple the broken statue of a god spoke a mysterious language. For me this vision is always accompanied by a feeling of cold, as if I had been touched by a winter wind from a distant, unknown country. The time? It is the frigid hour of dawn on a clear day, towards the end of spring. Then the still glaucous depth of the heavenly dome dizzies whoever looks at it fixedly; he shudders and feels himself drawn into the depths as if the sky were beneath his feet; so the boatman trembles as he leans over the gilded prow of the bark and stares at the blue abyss of the broken sea. Then like someone who steps from the light of day into the shade of a temple and at first cannot see the whitening statue, but slowly its form appears, ever purer, slowly the feeling of the primordial artist is reborn in me. He who first carved a god, who first wished to *create* a god. And then I wonder if the idea of imagining a god with human traits such as the Greeks conceived in art is not an eternal pretext for discovering many new sources of sensations.

The artists of the middle ages never succeed in expressing this feeling. This feeling, this sacred shudder of the artist who touches a stone or a fragment of wood, who polishes it, touches it, caresses it, with sacred feeling that the spirit of a god resides within it. Rare is the modern painter or sculptor who creates while gripped by such a joy. And yet I cannot otherwise conceive a work of art. Thought must so detach itself from all human fetters that all things appear to it anew—as if lit for the first time by a brilliant star.

If in the first light of dawn one can feel the shudder of death shot through with the shudder of eternity, receding to the end of everything, into the beginning of time, then many a covering and many a veil falls before this feeling. The medieval horror of death disappears, and with it the fear of the instant. One night, in the oppressive silence of the sleeping city I heard the resounding blows of a hammer upon planks. It seemed to me that somewhere a man was awake making a coffin. Then a dog howled in the night. Without reflecting I had a strange sensation that at that moment baneful stars moved in an unknown heaven.

Another night, a distant bell had just struck twelve when the sound of water running in a pail made me shiver as I lay on my bed. In the immense silence this noise seemed to me eternal—like the hammer blows I had already heard. This time, however, the sensation was more beautiful, and suddenly a face appeared before me, a face wearing the expression of *that which always is*. Once more my mind turned toward the past.

Tum Fauni similis circum pollercere coelum et languere simul tenebras et sidera pastor cernit . . .

Day is breaking. This is the hour of the enigma. This is also the hour of prehistory. The fancied song, the revelatory song of the last, morning dream of the prophet asleep at the foot of the sacred column, near the cold white simulacrum of a god.

One of the strangest and deepest sensations that prehistory has left with us is the sensation of foretelling. It will always exist. It is like an eternal proof of the senselessness of the universe. The first man must have seen auguries everywhere, he must have trembled at each step he took.

The wind rustles the oak leaves: it is the voice of a god which speaks, and the trembling prophet listens, his face bent towards earth.

Thinking of the temples dedicated to the sea gods, built along the arid coasts of Greece and Asia Minor, I have often conjured up those soothsayers tending to the voice of the waves receding from that ancient land. I have pictured them head and body wrapped in a chlamys, waiting for the mysterious revealing oracle. So also I once imagined the Ephesian, meditating in the first light of dawn under the peristyle of the Temple of Artemis of the hundred breasts.

And I think still of the enigma of the horse as a sea-god: I imagined him once in the darkness of a temple rising on the seashore, the talking, oracular steed that the god of the sea gave to the king of Argos. I imagined him fashioned in marble as clear and pure as a diamond, crouching on his hind legs like a sphinx, in his eyes and in the movement of his white neck all the enigma and the infinite nostalgia of the waves.

What is the trembling that the mystic priest feels as on a stormy night he draws close to the sacred oak?

In Rome the sense of prophecy is somehow larger: a feeling of infinite and distant grandeur inhabits it, the same feeling with which the Roman builder imbued his arcades, a reflection of the spasm of the infinite which the heavenly arch sometimes produces in man.

Often the prophecy was as awful as the cry of a dying god. Black clouds would come up, even to the towers of the city. In *Julius Caesar* Shakespeare has marvelously expressed such a moment, when he describes the sudden and terrible appearance of the lion to the Roman sentinel.

More distant and more beautiful is the song of the Italian poet:

Sed taciti durare boves tacitosque per omnes
pergere terribilem fugientes pone bubulum.

The first orator wants to lay out the limits of the city. The wandering herdsmen make fun of the man, who insists. With an iron sound a large furrow is opened. But the earth is arable only to draw a boundary. And suddenly, like a flash of lightning in a clear sky, the Olympian bird appears in the air. He gazes long and fixedly on the man's work. His wings spread under the sun's golden shower, he looks at the limiting plough, then disappears in the distance of the heavenly depths.

Hic ample sub sole datis immobilis alis
Forma aquila visa est opus observare dui, mox
defixis illue oculis se mergere coelo.—

Some few modern artists, among them the cubists, have freed themselves from the stupid Gothicism of French impressionism and seek an art at once more solid and more spiritual; a *more Romanesque* art. Their development is the reverse of that of the medieval architects. So much the better.

AN EXHIBITION IN FLORENCE OF SOME WORKS OF ANDREA DEL CASTAGNO

At the beginning of the fifteenth century in Florence, Donatello's naturalism had just woken Tuscan art from the deep mystic dream into which it had been sunk by the ascetic compositions of Giotto and his followers. The naïve visions and unhappy nightmares of deeply Christian thought were thus forever discarded. The saints now move more freely in pictures and frescoes, become less ecstatic, their glances turn towards earth and the things around them. No more the skies so strangely blue and deep, no more the solitary and melancholy landscapes which seem to await some miracle. Horizons become less vague; behind the virgins and martyrs rise beautiful, solid arches and sunlit pediments. This is the road down which walked the first Florentine artists of the Renaissance. In painting the study of reality was begun by Masaccio, who, one may say, achieved in color what Donatello achieved in marble and bronze. One of the most interesting artists of this period is Andrea del Castagno, whose life and work deserve to be better known.

This Florentine painter was a strange man, with an evil and melancholy expression, and an angular face. He was violent and simple, as skillful with pencil and brush as with club and dagger. His life, forever stained with blood by a murder, has something sad and brutal about it. Born in the first decade of the fifteenth century, in a little house called "il Castagno" in the village of "Mugello," a hamlet near Florence, he was still a child when his father died. Several years later he entered the service of an uncle whose sheep and goats he tended in the ravines and on the wooded hills of Tuscany. Thus he never knew the sweet pleasures and deep feeling of a family, those sentiments which shape and ennoble a man's soul. Always alone with his dog in the midst of his flocks, violent and suspicious, he often fought, throwing stones at the rogues he met along the road, and thus grew up into a strong and brutal man.

Then by chance, during a hot, stormy day, a naïve artistic vision turned him from the rude and somber life he had been leading: surprised by a shower while he watched his flocks, he took shelter in a tiny house hidden among cypresses and grape-vines, and there, in a bare, faintly lit room, he saw a man lovingly painting an altar-piece. This sight so impressed the shepherd that he stayed and watched the painter, and from that day on he began to draw the likenesses of men and animals on stones and walls. The peasants watched young Andrea's mania with curiosity, and a Florentine gentleman, Bernardetto de Medici, having taken notice of him, brought him to Florence, where, it is said, the shepherd of Mugello began his studies in the atelier of Masaccio. His talents were soon known. A biographer tells us of the terrible expressions of the heads of men and women that he painted. One of his first works was a fresco in the church of San Miniato al Monte: it showed St. Miniato and St. Cresci taking leave of their mother and father. In the monastery of San Benedetto there were also many paintings by Andrea, which were destroyed during the civil wars.

In the first cloister of the monastery of the Monaci degli Angeli, opposite the main portal, one can still admire his magnificent picture of the *Crucified*. Several of Castagno's best works may be found together in Florence, in a vast room belonging to the church of St. Apollonia. Apart from a Last Supper, painted on canvas, most of them are frescoes. There one may see several figures of famous Florentine men, painted for the palace of Pandolfo Pandolfini at Legnaia, near Florence. The figures are life size, simply painted, with a firm, hard outline; the predominating color is a dark red. The heads of the various people are very expressive, and several have that *espressione terribile* mentioned by his biographer. Such for instance, is the figure of Pippo Spano which seems like a portrait of Castagno himself. Solidly set on long legs covered with armor, the warrior grasps a long, curved two-edged sword with both hands. Curled hair covers a head tilted slightly to the left; haggard, staring eyes betray the ravages of thought. The whole is a vivid image of the Florentine of the time, constantly preoccupied by wars, plots and murders, always armed, on the watch, uneasy and suspicious. Faithfully and naïvely, the painter has recorded the marks these worries have left upon his countenance. Next to the figure of Pippo Spano stands that of Farinata degli Uberti, the chief of the Ghibellines, who in 1260 saved Florence from the destruction his fellows wished to wreak upon her as a revenge against the Guelphs: *Dominus Farinata de Uberti—sue patriae liberator*, says the Latin inscription underneath.

Nearby, the figure of a tetrarch: he holds a chief's baton in his right hand; a large white cloak is thrown over his armor; his head is turned a little to the left, as if he were listening to someone talk.

By his side one sees a strange figure of a virgin warrior with long blond tresses. She leans upon a lance held in her right hand, while a graceful gesture of her left hand lifts the long folds of the cloak that covers her cuirass.

This figure is followed by that of Dante, dressed in a purple robe, and holding the Divine Comedy. He holds out his left hand as if he were explaining some obscure passage of his work. Posed in the same position is a portrait of Petrarch, draped in an immense red cloak that also covers his head in a hood. Next to him Boccaccio, dressed in white, shows a book that he presses against his breast.

But the most striking painting is the *Last Supper*, whose composition is very different from other, much more famous versions of the same subject. The whole canvas* has a certain classic flavor, and is far from mystical. In a large room decorated in green and rose marble and flanked by two crouching sphinxes, the twelve apostles with Christ at the center are seated at a long table covered with a white cloth. All have a calm and pensive air, and one would imagine it to be a group of Greek philosophers come together to discuss the enigmas of life and the universe. A soft and even light shines through two windows on the left. The apostle John has sunk down on the table, his head in his arms, in an attitude of resigned sorrow. St. Thomas, his head lifted and his chin on his hand, looks towards heaven and seems gnawed by doubt. Judas, seated on the other side of the table, his hair as black as ebony and his skin a bilious yellow, appears as an evil spirit menacing the peace and calm of the gathering.

The *Pietà* is another strange and original fresco; its composition is simple but filled with pain and sorrow. The Virgin differs from all other pietàs. Castagno has painted a pale Christ with closed eye, who seems more faint then dead. Two angels, holding him by the arms, lay him gently at rest in a tomb decorated with sculpture.

His biographer tells us that Castagno was very jealous of a painter then famous in Florence, Domenico Veneziano, who had been called to Tuscany because of his new method of painting in oils. In the sacristy of Santa Maria di Loreto he and Piero della Francesca painted figures of a rare beauty which had given him a reputation in Florence. Castagno pretended friendship for Domenico, and the latter, a good and simple soul, became fond of him. Domenico used to sing while he accompanied himself on the lute, and on clear moonlit nights the two painters wandered in the silent streets of the city and often sang serenades under the windows of their *donne*. Finally Domenico revealed to Castagno the secret of his method of painting in oils. But Castagno, thinking that his colleague stood in the way of his own fame, hated him more and more, and the idea of murder began to fix itself in his mind. One summer evening the artists were working together as was their wont; and since the night was fine Domenico took his lute and invited his friend to go out with him. But Castagno refused, saying he had some drawings to finish, and Domenico went out alone. Andrea watched him from his window, and as soon as he saw that he had gone some distance, he put on a mask, armed himself with a heavy club with lead balls, ran and hid behind a wall. Then, as the unhappy Domenico came quietly home, he leaped upon him, struck him several terrible blows, burst open his belly, broke his lute, and then, as if nothing had happened, he went home and resumed the work he had interrupted. When some people who had been attracted by the cries of the wounded man called Andrea, he pretended to be terribly distressed by the misfortune of his friend, and holding him in his arms he cried out, weeping, "alas my brother, alas my brother," until the unhappy painter had breathed his last. No one would ever have thought of murder, if Castagno, on his deathbed, had not confessed his guilt.†

In 1478, after the Pazzi family and other conspirators had killed Giuliano de, Medici and badly wounded his brother Lorenzo in the church of Santa Maria del Fiore, the Signoria decided that all the plotters should be painted upon the wall of the Podestà as traitors. This fresco was proposed to Castagno, he accepted it with enthusiasm, and carried it out in an excellent work portraying all the traitors hung by the feet and contorted in strange positions. From that time on, he was nicknamed Andrea degli Impiccati (Andrea of the Hanged Men).

GIORGIO DE CHIRICO

* Castagno's *Last Supper* is a fresco, and therefore, of course, not on canvas. Ed.

† This story is now widely thought to be apocryphal. Ed.

MEDITATIONS OF A PAINTER
WHAT THE PAINTING OF THE FUTURE MIGHT BE

What will the aim of future painting be? The same as that of poetry, music and philosophy: to create previously unknown sensations; to strip art of everything routine and accepted, and of all subject-matter, in favor of an esthetic synthesis; completely to suppress man as a guide, or as a means to express symbol, sensation or thought, once and for all to free itself from the anthropomorphism that always shackles sculpture; to see everything, even man, in its quality of *thing*. This is the Nietzschean method. Applied to painting, it might produce extraordinary results. This is what I try to demonstrate in my pictures.

When Nietzsche talks of the pleasure he gets from reading Stendhal, or listening to the music from Carmen, one feels, if one is sensitive, what he means: the one is no longer a book, nor the other a piece of music, each is a *thing* from which one gets a sensation. That sensation is weighed and judged and compared to others more familiar, and the most original is chosen.

A truly immortal work of art can only be born through revelation. Schopenhauer has, perhaps, best defined and also (why not) explained such a moment when in *Parerga und Paralipomena* he says, "To have original, extraordinary, and perhaps even immortal ideas, one has but to isolate oneself from the world for a few moments so completely that the most commonplace happenings appear to be new and unfamiliar, and in this way reveal their true essence." If instead of the birth of *original, extraordinary, immortal* ideas, you imagine the birth of a work of art (painting or sculpture) in an artist's mind, you will have the principle of revelation in painting.

In connection with these problems let me recount how I had the revelation of a picture that I will show this year at the *Salon d'Automne*, entitled *Enigma of an Autumn Afternoon*. One clear autumnal afternoon I was sitting on a bench in the middle of the Piazza Santa Croce in Florence. It was of course not the first time I had seen this square. I had just come out of a long and painful intestinal illness, and I was in a nearly morbid state of sensitivity. The whole world, down to the marble of the buildings and the fountains, seemed to me to be convalescent. In the middle of the square rises a statue of Dante draped in a long cloak, holding his works clasped against his body, his laurel-crowned head bent thoughtfully earthward. The statue is in white marble, but time has given it a gray cast, very agreeable to the eye. The autumn sun, warm and unloving, lit the statue and the church façade. Then I had the strange impression that I was look   at all these things for the first time, and the composition of my picture came to my mind's eye. Now each time I look at this painting I again see that moment. Nevertheless the moment is an enigma to me, for it is inexplicable. And I like also to call the work which sprang from it an enigma.

Music cannot express the *non plus ultra* of sensation. After all, one never knows what music is about. After having heard any piece of music the listener has the right to say, and can say, what does this mean? In a profound painting, on the contrary, this is impossible: one must fall silent when one has penetrated it in all its profundity. Then light and shade, lines and angles, and the whole mystery of volume begin to talk.

The revelation of a work of art (painting or sculpture) can be born of a sudden, when one least expects it, and also can be stimulated by the sight of something. In the first instance it belongs to a class of rare and strange sensations that I have observed in only one modern man: Nietzsche. Among the ancients perhaps (I say perhaps because sometimes I doubt it) Phidias, when he conceived the plastic form of Pallas Athena, and Raphael, while painting the temple and the sky of his *Marriage of the Virgin* (in the Brera in Milan), knew this sensation. When Nietzsche talks of how his *Zarathustra* was conceived, and he says "I was *surprised* by Zarathustra," in this participle—surprised—is contained the whole enigma of sudden revelation.

When on the other hand a revelation grows out of the sight of an arrangement of objects, then the work which appears in our thoughts is closely linked to the circumstance that has provoked its birth. One resembles the other, but in a strange way, like the resemblance there is between two brothers, or rather between the image of someone we know seen in a dream, and that person in reality; it is, and at the same time it is not, that same person; it is as if there had been a slight transfiguration of the features. I believe that as from a certain point of view the sight of someone in a dream is a proof of his metaphysical reality, so, from the same point of view, the revelation of a work of art is the proof of the metaphysical reality of certain chance occurrences that we sometimes experience in the way and manner that *something* appears to us and provokes in us the image of a work of art, an image, which in our souls awakens surprise—sometimes, meditation —often, and always, the joy of creation.

THE SONG OF THE STATION

Little station, little station, what happiness I owe you. You look all around, to left and right, also behind you. Your flags snap distractedly, why suffer? Let us go in, aren't we already *numerous enough?* With white chalk or black coal let us trace happiness and its enigma, the enigma and its affirmation. Beneath the porticoes are windows, from each window an eye looks at us, and from the depths voices call to us. *The happiness of the station* comes to us, and goes from us transfigured. Little station, little station, you are a divine toy. What distraught Zeus forgot you on this square—geometric and yellow—near this limpid, disturbing fountain. All your little flags crackle together under the intoxication of the luminous sky. Behind walls life proceeds like a catastrophe. What does it all matter to you?

Little station, little station, what happiness I owe you.

THE MYSTERIOUS DEATH

The steeple clock marks half past twelve. The sun is high and burning in the sky. It lights houses, palaces, porticoes. Their shadows on the ground describe rectangles, squares, and trapezoids of so soft a black that the burned eye likes to refresh itself in them. What light. How sweet it would be to live down there, near a consoling portico or a foolish tower covered with little multicolored flags, among gentle and intelligent men. Has such an hour ever come? What matter, since we see it go!

What absence of storms, of owl cries, of tempestuous seas. Here Homer would have found no songs. A hearse has been waiting forever. It is black as hope, and this morning someone maintained that during the night it still waits. Somewhere is a corpse one cannot see. The clock marks twelve thirty-two; the sun is setting; it is time to leave.

A HOLIDAY

They were not many, but joy lent their faces a strange expression. The whole city was decked with flags. There were

flags on the big tower which rose at the end of the square, near the statue of the great king-conqueror. Banners crackled on the lighthouse, on the masts of the boats anchored in the harbor, on the porticoes, on the museum of rare paintings.

Towards the middle of the day *they* gathered in the main square, where a banquet had been set out. There was a long table in the center of the square.

The sun had a terrible beauty.

Precise, geometric shadows.

Against the depth of the sky the wind spread out the multicolored flags of the great red tower, which was of such a consoling red. Black specks moved at the top of the tower. They were gunners waiting to fire the noon salute.

At last the twelfth hour came. Solemn. Melancholic. When the sun reached the center of the heavenly arch a new clock was dedicated at the city's railroad station. Everyone wept. A train passed, whistling frantically. Cannon thundered. Alas, it was so beautiful.

Then, seated at the banquet, they ate roast lamb, mushrooms and bananas, and they drank clear, fresh water. Throughout the afternoon, in little separate groups, they walked under the arcades, and waited for the evening to take their repose.

That was all.

African sentiment. The arcade is here forever. Shadow from right to left, fresh breeze which causes forgetfulness, it falls like an enormous projected leaf. But its beauty is in its line: enigma of fatality, symbol of the intransigent will.

Ancient times, fitful lights and shadows. All the gods are dead. The knight's horn. The evening call at the edge of the woods: a city, a square, a harbor, arcades, gardens, an evening party; sadness. Nothing.

One can count the lines. The soul follows and grows with them. The statue, the meaningless statue had to be erected. The red wall hides all that is mortal of infinity. A sail; gentle ship with tender flanks; little amorous dog. Trains that pass. Enigma. The happiness of the banana tree: luxuriousness of ripe fruit, golden and sweet.

No battles. The giants have hidden behind the rocks. Horrible swords hang on the walls of dark and silent rooms. Death is there, full of promises. Medusa with eyes that do not see.

Wind behind the wall. Palm trees. Birds that never came.

THE MAN WITH THE ANGUISHED LOOK

In the noisy street catastrophe goes by. He had come there with his anguished look. Slowly he ate a cake so soft and sweet it seemed he was eating his heart. His eyes were very far apart.

What do I hear? Thunder rumbles in the distance, and everything trembles in the crystal ceiling; it is a battle. Rain has polished the pavement: summer joy.

A curious tenderness invades my heart: oh man, man, I want to make you happy. And if someone attacks you I will defend you with a lion's courage and a tiger's cruelty. Where do you wish to go; speak. Now the thunder no longer rumbles. See how the sky is pure and the trees radiant.

The four walls of the room broke him and blinded him. His icy heart melted slowly: he was perishing of love. Humble slave, you are as tender as a slaughtered lamb. Your blood runs on your tender beard. Man, I will cover you if you are cold. Come up. Happiness will roll at your feet like a crystal ball. And all the *constructions* of your mind will praise you together. On that day, I too will commend you, seated in the center of the sun-filled square, near the stone warrior and the empty pool. And towards evening, when the lighthouse shadow is long on the jetty, when the banners snap, and the white sails are as hard and round as breasts swollen with love and desire, we will fall in each other's arms, and together weep.

THE STATUE'S DESIRE

"I wish at any cost to be alone," said the statue with the eternal look. Wind, wind that cools my burning cheeks. And the terrible battle began. Broken heads fell, and skulls shone as if they were of ivory.

Flee, flee toward the square and radiant city. Behind, devils whip me with all their might. My calves bleed horribly. Oh the sadness of the lonely statue down there. Beatitude.

And never any sun. Never the yellow consolation of the lighted earth.

It *desires.*
Silence.
It loves its strange soul. It has *conquered.*

And now the sun has stopped, high in the center of the sky. And in everlasting happiness the statue immerses its soul in the contemplation of its shadow.

There is a room whose shutters are always closed. In one corner there is a book no one has ever read. And there on the wall is a picture one cannot see without weeping.

There are arcades in the room where he sleeps. When evening comes the crowd gathers there with a hum. When the heat has been torrid at noon, it comes there panting, seeking the cool. But he sleeps, he sleeps, he sleeps.

What happened? The beach was empty, and now I see someone seated there, there on a rock. A *god* is seated there, and he watches the sea in silence. And that is all.

The night is deep. I toss on my burning couch. Morpheus detests me. I hear the sound of a carriage approaching from far off. The hoofs of the horse, a gallop, and the noise bursts, and fades into the night. In the distance a locomotive whistles. The night is deep.

The statue of the conqueror in the square, his head bare and bald. Everywhere the sun rules. Everywhere shadows console.

Friend, with vulture's glance and smiling mouth, a garden gate is making you suffer. Imprisoned leopard, pace within your cage, and now, on your pedestal, in the pose of a conquering king, proclaim your victory.

Selected Bibliography

The numerous bibliographies on de Chirico, although varying considerably in coverage and competence, make another extensive list unnecessary. Those on the artist specifically (bibl. 21, 27, 85, 100) and on Italian art in general (bibl. 69, 80, 88, 95) are listed below. In consultation with the author, whose comments are incorporated, the compiler has organized a working bibliography. References are restricted to those of proved value for the present publication, and to those which best serve the needs of the research student. With few exceptions, the citations below are accessible in the Museum Library. Entries are arranged as follows: Writings by de Chirico, Books on de Chirico, Articles on de Chirico, General Works and Bibliographies, Exhibitions and Catalogs. There are on deposit in the Museum Library copies of some items difficult to obtain in the original, specifically bibl. (*).

BERNARD KARPEL
Librarian of the Museum

WRITINGS BY DE CHIRICO

*1 Arnoldo Boecklin. *Il Convegno* 1 no. 4: 47–53 ill. May 1920.

2 Classicismo pittorico. *La Ronda* no. 7: 506–11 July 1920.

3 Commedia dell'arte moderna. 239 p. Rome, Traguardi, 1945. *By de Chirico and Isabella Far. Reprints most of the early articles written for "Valori Plastici" (bibl. 2, 5, 7, 8, 9, 12, 14, 16, 20), as well as "Estetica metafisica," "Max Klinger" and articles for later publications.*

4 Le fils de l'ingénieur. *Poligono* Mar 1931. *Also in bibl. 26.*

5 Gustave Courbet. 13 p. ill. Rome, Valori Plastici, 1925. *Essay translated in M. Evans "The Painter's Object," p. 127–35 (London, Howe, 1937).*

6 Hebdomeros, 252 p. Paris, Carréfour, 1929. *Italian edition: Milan, Bompiani, 1942. Extract in "Bifur" no. 2: 5–15 July 1929, "View" 4 no. 3: 80–82 Oct 1944, and C. H. Ford "A Night with Jupiter," p. 26–33 (N. Y., View, 1945).*

*7 Impressionismo. *Valori Plastici* 1 no. 6–10: 25–26 June–Oct 1919. *Also in Galleria des Milione Bollettino no. 61 1939.*

8 Une lettre de Chirico. *Littérature* (n. s.) no. 1: 11–13 Mar 1 1922. *Explains to Breton his decision to abandon the early "metaphysical" style.*

*9 La mania del seicento. *Valori Plastici* 3 no. 3: 60–62 1921.

10 Memorie della mia vita. 257 p. Rome, Astrolabio, 1945. *Last chapter published in "Portfolio" (Washington, D. C.) no. 4 1946.*

11 Mystery and creation. *London Bulletin* no. 6: 14 1938. *Text in English and French.*

*12 Noi metafisici. *Cronache d'Attualità* Feb 15 1919. *Article for first one-man show published in bulletin of the Casa d'Arte Bragaglia; reprinted in bibl. 3.*

*13 Une nuit. *La Révolution Surréaliste* 1 no. 5: 7 Oct 15 1925. *A poem.*

*14 Il ritorno al mestiere. *Valori Plastici* 1 no. 11–12: 15–19 Nov–Dec 1919.

15 Salve Lutetia. *Bulletin de l'Effort Moderne* no. 33: 7–12 Mar 1927.

*16 Il senso architettonico nella pittura antica. *Valori Plastici* 2 no. 5–6: 59–61 May–June 1920.

17 Statues, meubles et généraux. *Bulletin de l'Effort Moderne* no. 38: 3–6 Oct 1927.

*18 Sull'arte metafisica. *Valori Plastici* 1 no. 4–5: 15–18 Apr–May 1919.

19 Sur le silence. *Minotaure* no. 5: 31–32 ill. May 1934.

*20 Zeusi l'esploratore. *Valori Plastici* 1 no. 1: 10 Nov 1918.

BOOKS ON DE CHIRICO

21 CARRIERI, RAFFAELE. Giorgio de Chirico. 24 p. plus 51 plates ill. Milan, Garzanti, 1942. *Bibliography by G. Scheiwiller.*

22 [CHIRICO, GIORGIO DE]. 12 Opere de Chirico. 2 p. plus 12 plates. Rome, Valori Plastici [1919]. *"Precedeute da giudizi critici di Soffici, Apollinaire, Vauxcelles, Raynal, Blanche, Marx, Papini, Carrà, Charles." The first edition devoted to the early paintings. Reviewed by Breton (bibl. 40).*

23 FALDI, ITALO. Il Primo de Chirico. 94 p. ill. Venice, Alfieri, 1949. *Bibliography. The first Italian monograph on de Chirico's early period. Reviewed by Ragghianti (bibl. 60).*

24 FAR, ISABELLA. Giorgio de Chirico. 12 p. plus 37 plates. Rome, Bestetti, 1953. *Preface by M. Biancale. Text also in English. Also see bibl. 3.*

25 GAFFÉ, RENÉ. Giorgio de Chirico, le Voyant. 41 p. plus 23 plates. Brussels, La Boétie, 1946.

26 GEORGE, WALDEMAR. Chirico, avec des fragments littéraires de l'artiste. 39 p. ill. Paris, Chroniques du Jour, 1928. *Includes bibl. 4.*

27 LO DUCA, GIUSEPPE. Dipinti di Giorgio de Chirico. 2 ed. 41 p. plus 38 plates. Milan, Hoepli, 1945. *First edition, 1936. Extensive bibliography by G. Scheiwiller, p. 17–41.*

28 PICA, AGNOLDOMENICO. 12 Opere di Giorgio de Chirico. 3. ed. 18 p. plus 14 col. plates. Milan, Ed. del Milione, 1947. *First edition, 1944. Illustrations vary. Third edition issued with insert: English translation by L. Krasnik.*

29 SELECTION (Periodical). Giorgio de Chirico. 84 p. ill. Antwerp, Éditions Sélection, 1929. *Special number of Dec. 1929, issued as Cahier 8. Texts by Courthion, Bardi, de Chirico. Bibliography.*

30 SOBY, JAMES THRALL. The early Chirico. 120 p. ill. New York, Dodd, Mead, 1941. *Bibliography.*

31 TERNOVETZ, BORIS. Giorgio de Chirico. 28 p. ill. Milan, Hoepli, 1928. *Bibliography.*

32 VITRAC, ROGER. G. de Chirico et son oeuvre. 63 p. ill. Paris, Gallimard, 1927. *"Les Peintres français nouveaux, no. 29."*

ARTICLES ON DE CHIRICO

33 ACQUA, GIAN ALBERTO DELL'. La peinture métaphysique. *Cahiers d'Art* 25: 121–65 ill. 1950.

34 ALLOWAY, LAWRENCE. The early Chirico, the London Gallery. *Art News and Review* 1 no. 6: 5 ill. Apr 23 1949.

*35 APOLLINAIRE, GUILLAUME. [Reviews]. *Intransigeant* Feb 28, Mar 3 1914. *The first merely lists de Chirico among leading moderns; the second contains an enthusiastic paragraph on his work at the Salon des Indépendants.*

*36 APOLLINAIRE, GUILLAUME. [Reviews]. *Paris Journal* June 23, July 14, July 23, Aug 1 1914. *Merely lists de Chirico among outstanding artists, except on July 14, where Apollinaire quotes Soffici (bibl. 64) and adds his own praise.*

*37 APOLLINAIRE, GUILLAUME. [Reviews]. *Les Soirées de Paris* no. 18: 9 Nov 15 1913; no. 22: 186 Mar 15 1914. *The first points out de Chirico's works—"almost certainly for the first time"; the second contains an important description of the painter's art.*

38 APOLLONIO, UMBRO. La pittura metafisica alla XXIV Biennale. *Le Arti Belle* no. 14–15: 35–43 ill. 1948.

39 BREDDO, GASTONE. Giorgio de Chirico, pittore surrealista. *Lettere ed Arti* no. 1: 36–39 ill. Sept 1945.

40 BRETON, ANDRÉ. Giorgio de Chirico—12 tavole in fototipia. *Littérature* 2 no. 2: 28 Jan 1920. *Review of bibl. 22.*

41 CASTELFRANCO, GIORGIO. Giorgio de Chirico. *Der Cicerone* 16 no. 10: 459–63 ill. May 1924. *Also in "Jahrbuch der Jungen Kunst", p. 128–133, 1924.*

42 COLLIS, MAURICE. Giorgio de Chirico. *Art News and Review* 1 no. 8: 1,6 ill. May 21 1949.

43 COURTHION, PIERRE. Giorgio de Chirico. *Cahiers d'Art* 1 no. 5: 115–116 ill. June 1926.

44 DÄUBLER, THEODOR. Neueste Kunst in Italien. *Der Cicerone* 12 no. 9: 349–54 ill. May 1920. *Also in "Jahrbuch der Jungen Kunst", p. 141–146, 1920.*

45 DELBANCO, GUSTAV. Henry Moore und Giorgio de Chirico. *Die Weltkunst* 5 no. 17: 15 Apr 26 1931.

46 GIBSON, W. Giorgio di Chirico. *The Enemy* 1 no. 1: 9–17 Jan 1927.

47 GOODRICH, LLOYD. Giorgio de Chirico. *The Arts* 15: 4–10 ill. Jan 1929.

*48 MANDIARGUES, ANDRE PIEYRE DE. La cité métaphysique. *Disque Vert* no. 5 1925?

49 MELVILLE, ROBERT. The visitation—1911–1917. *London Bulletin* no. 18–20: 7–9 ill. 1940.

50 MINOTAURE. no. 5 May 1934, no. 8 June 1936, no. 10 Winter 1937, no. 12–13 May 1939. *Illustrative material; texts by Tériade, Breton, etc.*

*51 MORISE, MAX. A propos de l'exposition Chirico. *La Révolution Surréaliste* 1 no. 4: 31–32 July 15 1925. *At the Galerie de l'Effort moderne.*

52 MOTHERWELL, ROBERT. Notes on Mondrian & Chirico. *VVV* (New York) no. 1: 59–61 1942.

53 NIBBI, G. G. de Chirico. *Art in Australia* 4 no. 1: 60–61, 86 ill. Mar–May 1941.

*54 PISIS, FILIPPO DE. Carlo Carrà—G. de Chirico. *Gazzetta Ferrarese* Feb 12 1918. *The critic wrote this review without knowing that only Carrà was exhibited.*

255

55 PISIS, FILIPPO DE. La cosidetta arte metafisica. *Emporium* 88: 257–65 ill. Nov 1938.

*56 PISIS, FILIPPO DE. Disegni di Giorgio de Chirico. *La Provincia di Ferrara* 19 no. 23: 1 Feb 21 1919.

*57 PISIS, FILIPPO DE. Esposizione di pittura moderna a Viareggio: Carlo Carrà—Giorgio de Chirico. *Fronte Interno* Aug 30 1918.

*58 PISIS, FILIPPO DE. Il pittore Giorgio de Chirico. *Gazzetta Ferrarese* Oct 11 1916.

59 RAGGHIANTI, CARLO L. Giorgio de Chirico. *La Critica d'Arte* 1 no. 1: 52–60 Oct 1935.

60 RAGGHIANTI, CARLO L. Il primo de Chirico. *La Critica d'Arte* 8 no. 4: 325–331 ill. Nov 1949. *Review of Faldi (bibl. 23) and "proposes a relationship between late eighteenth and early nineteenth century neo-classicism in German and French architecture and de Chirico's handling of architectural subjects in his early paintings of Italian squares."*

*61 RIBEMONT-DESSAIGNES, G. Giorgio de Chirico. *Les Feuilles Libres* 7 no. 43: 41–43 ill. May–June 1926. *Reproduces early de Chiricos in Marcel Ravel collection.*

62 RIBEMONT-DESSAIGNES, G. Giorgio di Chirico. *Documents* 2 no. 6: 336–345 ill. 1930.

*63 LA RÉVOLUTION SURRÉALISTE (Paris). Edited by Pierre Naville and Benjamin Péret. No. 1, Dec 1924—No. 12, Dec 1929. *See also bibl. 66.*

*64 SOFFICI, ARDENGO. Italiani all'estero. *Lacerba* 2 no. 13: 206–7 July 1 1914. *Probably first tribute to de Chirico by a countryman; translated by Apollinaire in "Paris Journal," July 14 1914 in review: Les Arts-Nouveaux peintres.*

65 SOLMAN, JOE. Chirico—father of surrealism. *Art Front* 2 no. 2: 6–7 Jan 1936. *Review of Matisse Gallery show.*

*66 Sur les possibilités irrationnelles de pénétration et d'orientation dans un tableau. *Le Surréalisme au Service de la Révolution* no. 5–6: 13–16 ill. May 11 1933. *On de Chirico's "The Enigma of a Day;" a questionnaire to leading artists and writers titled: Recherches expérimentales.*

67 VALESECCHI, MARCO. Una pagina per de Chirico. *Lettere ed Arte* 2 no. 4: 14–17, 21 ill. Apr 1946.

68 VITRAC, ROGER. Giorgio de Chirico. *Littérature* (nouvelle serié) no. 1: 9–11 Mar 1922.

GENERAL WORKS AND BIBLIOGRAPHIES

69 AESCHLIMANN, ERARDO. Bibliografia del Libro d'Arte Italiano, 1940–1952. p. 16, 17, 93, 98, 99, 102, 112, 118, 127, 151, 241, 245. Rome, Bestetti, 1952.

*70 ARAGON, LOUIS. La Peinture au Défi. 32 p. ill. Paris, Galerie Goemans, 1930. *"Exposition de collages . . . mars 1930."*

71 BASLER, ADOLPHE. Le Cafard aprés la Fête. p. 57–59 Paris, Jean Budry, 1929. *Barnes preface for Chirico exhibition (1926), originally issued in Guillaume catalog (*).*

72 BERNARD, CHARLES [and others]. Peintres Belges Contemporains. p. 157–61 ill. Brussels, Éditions Lumière, 1945. *E. L. T. Mesens on Magritte, who tells how de Chirico's "Song of Love" (1914) turned him toward surrealist painting.*

73 BILLY, ANDRÉ. Apollinaire Vivant. 119 p. Paris, La Sirène, 1923.

74 BRETON, ANDRÉ. Entretiens, 1913–1952. 317 p. Paris, Gallimard, 1952.

75 BRETON, ANDRÉ. Les Pas Perdus. 222 p. Paris, Gallimard, 1924.

76 BRETON, ANDRÉ. Le Surréalisme et la Peinture. 72 p. ill. Paris, Gallimard, 1928. *Enlarged edition (199 p.): New York, Brentano's, 1945.*

77 CAIROLA, STEFANO. Arte Italiano del Nostro Tempo. p. 26–28 ill. Bergamo, Instituto d'Arte Grafiche, 1946.

78 CARRA, CARLO. La Mia Vita. 2. ed. Milan, Rizzoli, 1945. *First edition: Rome, Longanesi, 1943.*

79 CARRA, CARLO. Pittura Metafisica. 264 p. Milan, Il Balcone, 1945. *First edition: Florence, Vallecchi, 1919.*

80 CARRIERI, RAFFAELE. Pittura, Scultura d'Avanguardia in Italia. 245 p. ill. Milan, Conchiglia, 1950. *"La pittura metafisica," p. 101–144. Extensive bibliographies.*

*81 DICTIONNAIRE ABRÉGÉ DU SURRÉALISME. 84 p. Paris, Galerie Beaux-Arts, 1938. *Supplement: "Exposition Internationale du Surréalisme," Jan–Feb 1938.*

82 EINSTEIN, CARL. Die Kunst des 20. Jahrhunderts. 656 p. Berlin, Propyläen-Verlag, 1931. *First edition, 1926; second edition, 1928.*

83 ELUARD, PAUL. Donner à Voir. 5. ed. p. 117–120, 183. Paris, Gallimard, 1939. *Quotes from de Chirico mss: (Appendix A).*

84 GIEDION-WELCKER, CAROLA. Poètes à l'Ecart; Anthologie der Abseitigen. p. 199–204 ill. Bern-Bümpliz, Benteli, 1946. *Bibliography.*

85 HUYGHE, RENÉ. Histoire de l'Art Contemporain: la Peinture. p. 483–491 ill. Paris, Alcan, 1935. *Vincenzo Costantini's "La peinture italienne après le futurisme" and bibliographies originally published in "L'Amour de l'Art" 15: 483–91 Nov 1934.*

*86 LONDON BULLETIN. no. 6: 12–19 ill. Oct 1938. *Poem and text by F. Brockway; London Gallery catalog (Oct 14–Nov 12); Chirico text (bibl. 11). Additional illustrations and essays in no. 3: 13, no. 6: 15–18, no. 14: 10–12 (Lecomte text), no. 18–20: cover, 7–9 (Melville text).*

87 NEW YORK. MUSEUM OF MODERN ART. Fantastic Art, Dada, Surrealism. Ed. by Alfred H. Barr, Jr; essays by Georges Hugnet. 3. ed. 271 p. ill. New York, 1947. *Issued 1936 as catalog and text for an exhibition; bibliography.*

88 NEW YORK. MUSEUM OF MODERN ART. Twentieth-Century Italian Art, by James Thrall Soby and Alfred H. Barr, Jr. 144 p. ill. New York, 1949. *Catalog of an exhibition; critical essays; bibliography.*

*89 LE NÉOCLASSICISME DANS L'ART CONTEMPORAIN. 98 p. ill. Rome, Valori Plastici [1923]. *Essays by Carlo Carrà and others.*

90 PISIS, FILIPPO DE. La Città dalla 100 Meraviglie. Rome, Casa d'Arte Bragaglia [192?]. *Dated 1924 by G. Scheiwiller, this is an important work on Ferrara and "metaphysical" subjects.*

91 PISIS, FILIPPO DE. Pittura Moderna: Conferenza. Ferrara, Taddei-Neppi, 1918. *Copy not available.*

92 PISIS, FILIPPO DE. Prose e Articoli. p. 166–178. Milan, Il Balcone, 1947. *Reprints early articles; also parts of bibl. 90.*

93 RAYNAL, MAURICE. Modern Painting. p. 197–203, 297–8 ill. Geneva, Skira, 1953. *Bibliography. Similar coverage in "History of Modern Painting, v. 3: From Picasso to Surrealism" p. 104–5, 107–10, 193 (1950).*

94 SAN LAZZARO, GUALTIERI DI. Painting in France. p. 74–87. New York, Philosophical Library, 1949. *Revised edition of "Cinquanti'Anni dei Pittura Moderna in Francia" (Rome, Danesi, 1945).*

95 SCHEIWILLER, GIOVANNI. Arte Moderna Italiana. 73 leaves [Milan, 1949]. *A typescript bibliography compiled on the occasion of the Italian exhibition (bibl. 88). Copy in the Museum of Modern Art Library. The most extensive bibliographies on Chirico, compiled by Scheiwiller, have been published in bibl. 21, 27.*

96 SOBY, JAMES THRALL. After Picasso. p. 83–85 et passim. ill. New York, Dodd, Mead, 1935.

97 SOFFICI, ARDENGO. Scoperte e Massacri. 2. ed. Florence, Vallecchi, 1929. *"Written July 1914;" first edition 1919.*

98 VALORI PLASTICI (Rome). Edited by Mario Broglio. 1 no. 1 (Nov 15, 1918)–3 no. 5 (Oct 1921). *Invaluable record of the metaphysical group; articles on and by Chirico, Carrà, Soffici, etc.; good plates.*

99 VENTURI, LIONELLO. Italian Painting from Caravaggio to Modigliani. p. 142–51; 170 ill. Geneva, New York, Skira, 1952. *Bibliography.*

100 VOLLMER, HANS. Allgemeines Lexikon der bildenden Künstler des XX. Jahrhunderts. vol. 1, p. 434. Leipzig, Seemann, 1953. *Bibliography.*

101 WYSS, DIETER. Der Surrealismus. 88 p. ill. Heidelberg, Schneider, 1950. *Bibliography.*

102 ZERVOS, CHRISTIAN. Histoire de l'Art Contemporain. p. 383–392 ill. Paris, Cahiers d'Art, 1938.

103 WILD, DORIS. Moderne Malerei. p. 208–14 ill. Konstanz, Europa, 1950.

EXHIBITIONS AND CATALOGS

1912, PARIS: Salon d'Automne. *Exhibits "L'Énigme de l'oracle," "L'Énigme d'un aprés-midi d'automne," "Portrait de l'artiste par lui-même" (no. 368–370).*

1913, PARIS: Salon d'Automne. *Exhibits "Portrait de Mme L. Gartzen," "La Mélancolie d'une belle journée," "La Tour rouge," "Étude" (no. 399–402).*

1913, PARIS: Salon des Indépendants. *Exhibits "La Mélancolie du départ," "L'Énigme de l'heure," "L'Énigme de l'arrivée et de l'après-midi" (no. 627–629).*

1914, PARIS: Salon des Indépendants. *Exhibits "La Nostalgie de l'infini," "Joies et énigmes d'une heure étrange," "L'Énigme d'une journée" (no. 682–684).*

1919, ROME: Casa d'Arte Bragaglia (*Early winter*). *See bibl. 12.*

1925, PARIS: Galerie de l'Effort Moderne (*July*). *See bibl. 51.*

1926, PARIS: Chez Paul Guillaume (*June 4–12; over 30 early works*). *Preface to catalog by Albert C. Barnes, also in bibl. 71.*

1928, PARIS: Galerie Surréaliste (*Feb 15–Mar 1; 18 early works*). *Preface to catalog by Louis Aragon.*

1935, NEW YORK: Pierre Matisse Gallery (*Nov 19–Dec 21; 26 works from 1908–1918*).

1936, LONDON: New Burlington Galleries. International Surrealist Exhibition (*June 11–July 4; nos. 46–57 by Chirico*).

1936, LONDON: London Gallery (*Oct 14–Nov 12; 14 paintings, 4 drawings*). *See bibl. 86.*

1937, LONDON: Zwemmer Gallery (*To June 30; 10 works in Chirico-Picasso exhibition*).

1939, MILAN: Galleria del Milione (*Oct 26–Nov 15; 18 "metaphysical" paintings*). Bollettino 61 also contains bibl. 7. *Reviewed in "Arti" 2: 118–21 Dec 39.*

1940, NEW YORK: Pierre Matisse Gallery (*Oct 22–Nov 23; "Early paintings"*).

1943, NEW YORK: Art of This Century (*Oct 5–Nov 6; 18 "Masterworks of early De Chirico"*). *Mimeographed checklist.*

1948, VENICE: XXIV Biennale. (*Sale III–IV: Tre Pittori italiani dal 1910 al 1920: Carrà, De Chirico, Morandi; preface by F. Arcangeli*).

Index